BRITISH POETRY REVIEW 1993

MAST PUBLICATIONS

First published in Great Britain in 1993 by

Mast Publications, 31 Beaufort Gardens, Knightsbridge, London SW3 1QH

British Poetry Review 1993

Edited by
Steve James

ISBN 1-898322-01-5

Published, typeset and distributed by
Mast Publications

Printed and bound by
Input Typesetting Ltd, Wimbledon, London SW19 8DR

Goodbye McLeod
Jean Cunningham

You are the sky, the moon and the stars,
You are the grass that sways in the breeze,
You are the birds flying so high,
You are the shaded leaves on the trees.
You are the rain that dampens the skin,
You are the sea with its changing scenes,
You are the moors, mountains and hills,
You are the canals and rivers and streams.
You are the seasons that come and go,
You are the rose so ethereal and white,
You are the hay, the corn and the harvest,
You are the morning, noon and night.
You are forever.

To Christine
Julia Yardley

You're in God's lovely garden now
You walk through fields of flowers
You stand 'neath trees so beautiful
You sit in shaded bowers
He must have felt you worthy
To have you there so young
To leave us here to mourn you
Your earthly life unsung
We hold you close within our hearts
And there you will remain
Your presence felt throughout our days
Until we meet again.

M6, Junction 7
David Haden

Late afternoon, August.

In the fluting advance of a storm
flowers burn up their own colour
under a sky which finds the spot
where no-one looks.

B-road, motorway, pylons, bright new houses

shoulder up to a headland
of nowhere. Flashpoint of speed
outstripping its own distance,
a molten tiding, down

to the deadlocked cities.

The swung heat of afternoon.
Ruled trajectories hide under
wasp husks. Pylons
ride their geometries

to a static horizon.

Lonely half-place, peopled for seconds
by a brief community
of flatland glances;
yet everywhere the hand of man

shines out against the closing thunder.

Warwick
Fred Holland

Drinking coffee in the room where we drank together
Once, months ago, now alone I sit and watch
The slim-waisted waitress come and go and I
Smile, admiring her innocent, friendly smile
While a fly which troubles and eludes her,
Buzzes near the cake-stand by the door.

I read my paper, nervous, full of recollections,
Disquiet, and I glance at the table
Where once we sat, briefly, that cold afternoon
When I ordered wrongly what I thought you liked,
And someone looked, perceiving us not to be
As well acquainted as one might suppose.

Was that why I came here this day, alone,
'To view a voiceless ghost'? Oh no, not that,
Surely, Yet why do I write of it thus, distantly,
Distinctly recalling, recording, rehearsing
The words I ought to have said, the moves
I ought to have made with quiet conviction.

Instead I sit here alone, sipping my coffee,
Smiling at the girl, glancing at my paper
And wondering if ever time and the girl
Will come together in my aberrant world;
Will she share my fantasies, her slim wrists
Suddenly showing as she pours me another cup?

The Lonely Child
Hilda Stagg

Please hold my hand the little child said
And hug me close before I go to bed
I have not the time the mother cried
To spend with you so go away and hide
Who is this child who needs to be consoled
To work through anger, fear and grief so cold
To find two arms to hold and keep her safe
To give a smile of love and not a look of hate
Someone to listen when she tries to tell
Of those who drove her to the brink of hell
Of how her body aches with tears unshed
The awful tears that fills the little head
She lives in me that who was used
For others pleasures broken and abused
Sometimes she needs to ask for care
So give her time, allow her to shed little tears
As she has held them back for many lonely years.

The Eternal Soldier
Arthur Howe

Alone we stand by sentinels of stone
and ponder on in silence, far from home

Are they at peace so far from Englands shore
or do they recall that half forgotten war

And do they understand the reason why
That fate had picked them as the ones to die

Did they believe that had to do what's right
or just the victims of a bloody fight

Was it for glory and a bugles clarion call
or fighting evil that would affect us all

Or maybe just another job to do
The ones that fought to see the whole thing through

The softly calming tread of time moves on
and all the clamour and the fury has now gone

No more do weeping women lonely stand
While others reach for that returning hand

We cannot comprehend the sight we see
The human price of war - now history

We will remember them

In memory of Lance Corporal John Nicholson
Died in action Dunkirk 1940

Choices
Patricia Rogers

I did not choose to love you.
I did not seek you out.
I did not wish to think of you
each day and night throughout.

Love comes sometimes unbidden

unnoticed till it's there.
And does not always bring about
great happiness to share.

Sometimes, it comes when you already have
Someone whose life you share
and you would rather not know the pain
of a new love again.

It would be oh! so easy
if love could be bought, or turned off like a tap
But those who've known deep love inside
feel it's not at all like that.

So please be patient, don't mock or be unkind.
In time, this pain will leave my mind
and Peace and Happiness I'll find.

Lights Of The City
Sue Williams

Lights of the City,
All twinkle and flair.
And the wind rushes inward,
With never a care.

The treetops are swaying,
All billowed and tossed.
And the poor man just stands there,
Bedraggled, and lost.

How yellow the floodlight,

How hardened the seat.
No comfort, or sanctuary,
No place for a sleep.

But what can you do,
When your journey, - is end.
With no welcoming home, or a fire,
Or, a friend.

Canny Cats
B J Bevan

I know three cats, all canny.
With cocked ears, eyes afire
They plan, acquire.
One rat-tat-tats doorknockers,
Makes important din
To be let in.
This small tiger paddles,
Steals drinks from dripping taps
With lazy laps.
And number two composes
Contemporary piano stuff
With feet and fluff.
Cat three is still, and wise,
Seizing comforts' chances
With sidelong glances.
Saucepan lids are lifted,
Curtains flung awry
For cats to spy.
These canny cats are mine -
Or, I should say I'm theirs,
Bless their hairs.

Birds
Howard Cheetham

Birds fly round the summer skies,
Wheeling and swooping before your eyes.
Ever moving, never at rest,
Flying North, South, East and West.

Soaring, diving, high and low,
Sometimes fast and sometimes slow.
In a flock or all alone.
Sometimes dropping like a stone.

As the light begins to fade
And sunlit paths recede in shade,
The birds come down and rest in trees,
Hedges, grassbanks, cliffs near seas.

The birds stay silent through the night,
Resting peacefully out of sight,
Waiting for the coming dawn
To greet with singing, a bright new morn.

The Long Road
Michael Latimer

The road leads off towards the watery sun
Sending ripples of frustration
Through my head

I look at the ground
Stones set in the caked earth

like jewels in a gaudy crown

The dirt is dented by the dozens of pounding boots
all seventeen miles up the road
in which even I melt into insignificance

The Boredom weighs down my limbs
more than the physical strain
as every minute counts as three

But I'll have to keep on walking
down the long road like everyone has to
one time or another.

The Unexplained.......
Freda Nicholson

Things happen to me called the unexplained,
Perhaps it's a gift, as I am not disarranged,
These beings just stand and don't say a word,
Am I dreaming, it's all so absurd,
I am not frightened in any way,
They are never here long and don't seem to stay,
Can I help, I think to myself,
Or shall I forget it and do something else,
Did I just conjure them up in my mind,
They are welcome to come if they be so inclined,
My Grannie and Uncle have come into view,
Are long since dead, I'm saying to you,
When you have read this, please stop to think,
Do these folk, just want to keep up a link,
So don't be afraid, look and maybe you will see,
The unexplained things that happen to me.

Soul Search For The Modern Marriage
C E Goodman

What does it; matter; living or non?
It has not happiness.
It is alive but does not live,
Breeding envy, competition and false hope.
Oh, deceitful electrons!

Upon my soul, that is where I live.
Blessed to think, but not to act
Upon my word!
Actions left to the less superior and all that Business.
Oh, conceitful spirit!

Who will marry one who has married so many already?

With spouses living or non, Plato, Dimnet, Eliot,
oneself above all,
The search for those hungry, lives in my heart.
Do not ask how our minds will meet,
But criticise the creativity. There you will find me in our
Solitude.
Oh, receiptful bliss!

"Congratulations and happiness to us both"

Fishing Fleet
Chris Dobson

The birds wheel and circle,
On knife-sharp wings
they dive and plummet,

Snatching the silver fishes
from the encircling nets.

Harsh cries cut the air
as on beating wings,
They climb.
They soar above the boats
and circle once more.

Nothing escapes the birds.
Their diamond eyes see all
The bobbing boats,
The tiny men,
The glittering shoals of herring.

Where Does The River Go
J Hodgkins

Where does the river go?
From prancing spring to diesel flow
Kingfisher, flash of turquoise blue
To dabbling duck of mottled hue
Reed beds and grassy banks
To factory wall and rotting planks
Salmon leaping to the skies
Stickleback midst the rubbish lies
Sparkling stream from ice and snow
Does to a stagnant monster grow

A November Morn
V F Oakes

Oh, cold and damp, November morn
The month that heralds winters dawn,
When leaves do'th change to autumn red
Then fall, to leave the tree as dead.
When creatures hibernate underground,
And Jack Frost whitens all around,
When icicles hang as daggers poised,
Dripping tears for summers skies.

Oh, cold and damp November day
With winters suns that will not stay
But briefly shines, then quickly sets
With weakened glow and shamed regrets,
Giving way to winters birth
As frosty dampness grips the earth,
All life encompassed, stands as dead,
As winters reaper ploughs ahead.

Oh, budding trees, born e're last spring
Oh, joyous songbird, that did sing,
Where hide you now - That I may seek
To share your song in a world now bleak,
A frozen world, where little do'th live,
That asks for all - yet nought will give,
A world that maketh all forlorn
On this cold, damp November morn.

Butterfly
B Bulmer

Emperors, peacocks, blue as sky
Browns and coppers flutter by
Caught on the breeze and tossed on high
Across the fields meander

Painted lady painted bright
Speckled wood in forest flight
Skippers, hairstreaks, marbled
white Borne by the wind to wander

What silken beauties summer brings
With dancing courtship on the wings
While chaffinch in the hedgerow sing
Whither do you wander

Admiral, brimstone, tortoiseshell
Drinking nectar from the well
Deep within the foxgloves bell
Where do you sleep, I ponder

Please come to me at any hour
Within my perfumed garden bower
Visit each and every open flower
While I will watch in wonder

The Lonely Captive
J P Hornett

Lest I forget, on this bright day
While here in my lonely room

I hear children at their play,
Hidden thoughts return
as secret laughter on the wind
echoing, half remembered dreams,
where valleys green, with golden sunshine glow
the soundless hills casting shadows
on a lake far far below,
My heart is stilled, in this tranquil land,
and my friend is peace.

Gently, still waters stir,
and in silence swoops a bird of prey
Time suspended, in a glistening spray,
His lonely captive a silent scream
disturbs my dreams and
I am left, bereft,
In the falling darkness
Where ghostly shadows fill my mind,
Till I find sleep, merciful sleep.

Camping In Greece
Michael Foster

Under the olive trees
Ten nations mingle,
Share toilets and ablutions,
Swap experiences.
No common language
But unspoken thoughts
Of friendly co-existence.
Three bikers set up camp
Beside flash motor caravans.

A hitcher stumbles in
And pitches tiny tent
Next to palatial family encampment.
Night 'silence time', not heeded everywhere,
Is here obeyed implicitly, unforced.
And over all the olive branches stir,
Politically neutral, shading equally
The rich, the poor, the stronger and the weak...

My Friend The Fun Deva
Isabel Hurney

My Fun Deva is my very good friend
Helps me laugh and smile no end
Anyone can have one it only takes a smile
Followed by a laugh - all makes life worthwhile.
Laughter is a tonic - takes away all the gloom
Makes the world a better place - lights up every room.
It's fun to see the humour spread
As faces light up - some quite red.
Let's make the world a happy place
And put a smile upon our face
Humour is a wondrous thing
Lots of happiness it will bring
To you and me - the rich and poor
Deva's knock on any door
To anyone who smiles and grins
The Fun Deva will soon be in
So let's be jolly, let's be bright
And everything will turn out right.

Coventry, Our New Cathedral
Mary Siddle

Vision upon vision, thought upon thought,
Sketching, planning, only to start anew,
Thinking of a task oft by dangers fraught,
Yet driven on with a hope in view, -
It has arisen, a building from the dust,
Amidst the City's bustle and its spires;
For the Glory of God to be? it must,
For strains of praise burst forth from its choirs;
And now the vision of this building grand
Is tangible, complete for all to see,
Yet very near old walls around still stand
Like sentinels to guard the way so free;
This then is where many souls can retreat,
And if right in heart can God in spirit meet!

The Gardener
Dominic Delve

So much rain,
So much growth,
So much pain through the window
Two knackered knees,
Two slicing eyes
Two blades side by side
Resting, nullified, accepting.

Cotswold Scene
Wendy Dedicott

Wheat peeps over the dry stone wall
And high above we hear larks call
Between the stones the bindweed creeps
And a lively weasel peeps
His bright eyes watch the knapweed blow
Dodging the insects flying show
Graceful scabious slowly wave
Bearded oats await their shave
Tractors drone in nearby fields
Farmers hoping for good yields
'Tis August yet the haws now show
Telling us Summer soon will go
Warm Summer days will now decrease
But Nature's round will never cease.

And No Birds...
Josie Davies

*"....the sedge is wither'd from the lake
And no birds sing." Keats.*

Imagine Summer without morning song -
tuneful alarum, sweet sonority
transcending sleep. Celestial throngs
trilling choice airs of feathered minstrelsy

have charmed the darkest dawn since Eden's birth
and from ten thousand leafy minarets
muezzins call the faithful round the earth
to celebrate, with dancing castanets

and clashing cymbals, each new day. But now
no blackbird sits atop the ancient pear,
no diva nightingale, and flowers bow
their heads and weep as pale ghosts stare

ashamed to see the desert they have made -
a wilderness where birds no longer sing,
no longer woo the wind with serenade -
and old men spend long days remembering.

Bonny Scotland
Wendy Scott

All over the heather,
The dew it has kissed
With mountain peaks, peeping
Above fingers of mist.

From up on the brae
I look down to the shore
And I drink in the sight till
I feel my eyes sore.

The beauty of Scotland
It fills me with pride
To think I am part of this
Beautiful Clyde.

Deep in my heart I can feel such a pleasure
The mountains, the river I glance at in leisure

For daily I feast upon beauties so rare

Changing colours and seasons the skyline so fair
'Bonny Scotland', How apt a phrase
Come visit this land let the sights here amaze.

The Refugee
Les Minter

An ill clad foot stumbles on unfamiliar terrain.
Arms pitch forward to save from hurt
And the precious bundle falls
To be scrambled for in anxious clutching.
Steadying hands offered in silent aid,
No word spoken in gratitude
But sad eyes meet in mutual understanding
Of a shared and hopeless misery.
No smile disturbs the gleaming courses
Where tears have cleansed their way
Through the layered dust of destruction.

Driven by whining bullet and indiscriminate shell,
Consuming fire where once was love,
The laughter of children and neighbour now turned foe.
Home where all therein made glad the heart of family
Is now a shattered dream, treasured in painful memory.
No purpose now in turning back
Yet forward is a path to chance
And the elusive hope of uncertainty.

Memories
Mavis Jackson

Off to the pictures I did go,
With big sisters Emmy and Flo,
Stopped at Granny's on the way back,
'Cos we felt like a little snack.
Crusts of bread spread thick with dripping
Enough to set your lips a-licking.
Singing and dancing back on our way,
Pretending to be Doris Day.
Dad was waiting, strap in hand and eyes ablaze
Seeking vengeance for our erring ways,
We all knew our dreadful fate,
Just because we were five minutes late.

Reaching Forty
Sally E Burton

You've done it, you've made it,
You've reached the big four - o
And now I have to warn you
To take things really slow
You're dressed up really snappy
And looking oh so slick
But please when you are going out
Don't forget your walking stick
Take things nice and easy
Have time for your own leisure
'Cause if you don't, I'm sure you know
You'll end up with with blood pressure.
If you get stuck, just give a yell

We're always there to help
And we don't take no notice
'Cause there's less hair than scalp
And if you're having trouble
Getting up the stairs
Give us a ring, we'll lend a hand
And show that someone cares
And if you follow my advice
And take things really slow
You'll of got the hang of it
For when you reach the big five - o

Janus, The Two Faced God
Mary Marriott

Janus, the two faced god,
Revolving through Time,
Striking off the years
In numbered succession.
Ring out the Old, we cry,
Closing the door on past hopes,
Unfulfilled endeavours.
Ring in the New, we proclaim,
Opening wide to unexplored horizons,
Untried resolutions.
Happy New Year, the world sings.
Welcome, Janus, with the bright new face.
Forget for a while the face waiting
In the shadows.
So the eternal paradox continues.

Winter
C Sandeman

Oft in the morning the fields are white
Encrusted and rimed by the frost in the night,
Or shining with dew, damp and sparkling bright
In Winter

The trees are standing bleak and bare,
Leafless arms upraised as in prayer,
A brisk chilly wind disturbs the air
In Winter.

The cats step tentatively out with dainty paws
They go reluctantly with good cause -
They much prefer to stay indoors
In Winter.

The birds a daily call now make
For we put out all the crumbs and cake
And water too, their thirst to slake
In Winter.

The squirrel no longer comes to play,
He is fast asleep in his cosy drey
The best place, by far, for him to stay
In Winter.

The fox curtails his wanderings
For the weather is cruel for all wild things
Nature seems to sleep while awaiting the Spring
In Winter.

Colour Blind
Shirley Monaco-Brown

Of all the colours in this world,
Our Father made them all,
Each little flower that opens,
Each tree short or tall,
The blue of the sky above,
And even sometimes grey,
When out of its very depth,
A storm is on the way.

Then the golden sun does shine,
To show the way is clear,
For the rainbow in the sky,
Will surely now appear
With colours there for all to see.

The yellow black, of the Bumble Bee,
Pink blossom of a flowering tree,
Many colours created He.

The minds of man - us His creation,
Is colour there within.
Creeds and colour make a Nation,
And when many look around
The colour of their mind is dim.

FOR THEY SEE

The different Nationalities,
And the colour of their skin.
But others then will look around,

23

Their mind colour and light,
For they see what the Father meant,
That we should mix and be content.

God mixed the colours of mankind,
'cos God is love and colour blind.

Vengeance
Dean Blades

The darkness turned to light
So began one mans fight,
For justice he sought
Or so he thought.

He worked out his plan
To revenge the man,
For the wrong he'd done
In the killing of his son.

He carried out his aim
Intended to kill not to maim,
Arrested the next day
With nothing to say.

Found guilty of course
But showed no remorse,
From his courtroom seat
Came the cry, "Revenge is sweet".

The Happy House
Winifred Heeley

A house
That is happy
Has welcome
On the mat
Any friends
Who care to call
Are invited in
To chat

The cushions
Will be rumpled
There'll be crumbs
On the floor
Who cares
About disorder
When friends
Come to the door

They are sure
To get a welcome
Because the house
Seems to say
How nice it is
To see you
I hope you've come
To stay

Rose Cottage
Philip W Whitbread

The sale sign, the broken gate
That muddy path, what a state!
The sagging roof, the broken tiles
Spelt out the work of future trials
The rotten frames the peeling walls
Ceilings dipped that said it all
Years of damp and dust and grime
This place had surely stopped in time!
But still a certain warmth and charm
An easy peace, a soothing calm
Set our minds and hearts as one
And souls determined we begun.
Steady work and honest sweat
Our goal in sight our target set
To mould and shape with grit and graft
To knit the present with the past
Now after years of loves hard labour
We can rest, reflect and savour
All the joy our home imparts
To ours and all our children's hearts.

Water
C W Vickers

Calm, calm descend, as water nears
And equilibrium return.
How could I stay away so long
From sea or lake or burn.
The little stream that brings the news

With playful jumps, cascades,
Often ends up in a pool
That's blue in many shades.
Oh, mighty sea that roars
With tides that match my waves,
Or glitter, glisten, gently lapping
Into sandy coastal caves.
I close my eyes and drink it in
Let the sound wash over me,
And when I open them again
All I can see is sea.

Home (Meet The Family)
Roger Bourne

I lend her twenty, she pays me back ten
Then I need a hundred and she says when
- Will I get *my* money back, Jack?

I've got to be thrifty
So I slip her fifty -
And hope she'll forget the rest.
Her *pest* of a sister
Was always a twister -
Says interest is due
A percentage or two
Would not go amiss for her sis.

Fifteen a week, I've hit a lean streak
It's the best I can do -
Would I lie to you?
But mother knows best

When put to the test
Pressed into action, can work to a fraction
Hand roll a joint, move a decimal point
- And rub in the ointment too!

The Day They Found Ol' Hubie Dry
Derek Rutherford

Was a strange Sunday, Sunday last.
Dawn greeted us with whispers
"The vampire's dead" the rumour said,
"He attacked ol' Hubie Driscoll."
Poor Hubie.

They found him in the gutter,
Dry as a bone amongst the cigarette ends and dirt.
Two holes torn in his ageing neck
An empty whisky bottle in his shirt.
Poor Hubie.

The way I see it: blurry eyes, hypnotized,
A dark stranger in a cloak,
"Have a swig," and the vampire did,
Johnny Walker from his throat.
Poor vampire.

He must have staggered through the night,
Full of Hubie's blood.
Sightless, legless, wingless, helpless,
Didn't know where his coffin was.
Poor vampire.

Come the morning, come the sun,
Dawn greeted us with whispers.
"Vampire's dead." the rumour said,
"He drank with Hubie Driscoll."

Yeah, was a strange Sunday, Sunday last.

Nightmare
K L Goulding

Life is just a series of quizzical dreams,
of hopes and asperations, and sometimes screams.
Chocolate doorknobs that melt in your hand,
leaving you trapped in a bucket of sand.

Your feet cannot move; and your eyes only stare,
at your past endeavours that got you nowhere.
Yet in that far away land that exists in your mind,
that haunts you in sleep and half closed eye.

The Dragon is coming in billows and fire,
to snuff out your life on a funeral pyre.
Beware the Dragon, don't let him in,
keep your mind in the light and free from sin.

Untitled
David Mountjoy

If a mans' mind is an island,
Then what of the sea,
Do we float on the surface,

Considering ourselves free?
What swims in the oceans
Of the unconscious id?
Are there mermaids and serpents
Or legions of squid.
Does man fear the water?
Does he fear its' depth?
Its unfathomable canyons,
Where Poseidon has wept.
Has he no desire, to be free of the land,
To release himself,
To the tides and the sand.
Will the present momentum,
For status and power,
Not hasten the arrival,
Of our judgement hour?
Will man himself, not sink his own rafts,
To begin once again,
The most ancient of crafts.
To descend this darkness, to the ocean floor
Confronting our egos'
In a sub-conscious war.

Freedom
Pat Thoirs

To travel life's road.
On a lonely quest
May be we're not always, looking our best.
Sad looking Scarecrows out in the fields.
Counting the miles to see what life yields.

Onward our journey.
Up to the isles.
Nothing to frown on.
Only our smiles
Happy to be the folk that we are.
Lucky, no city, better by far.

Friendly the folk
We meet on our way
Further we go now.
Each passing day.
Glad to he Happy
wonderfully Free
Just the best company
That's you and Me!

Old Glory
Les Poole

Lord tell me that you love me
When I answer to the call
Please put your arms around me
As the evening shadows fall.

Help me cross the great divide
To find the promised land
Or walk across the river
To where the water meets the sand.

There I'll board the glory train
In search of heavens gate
Where I know I'll find a welcome
If I arrive a little late.

For when Old Glory rounds the bend
I hope to find you there
With others who will welcome me
With love for me to share.

On reaching Lord, our journeys end
I found I was on loan
So Old Glory made a turn around
For you to send me home.

The Civilised Life
Philip Sanders

Locked, alarmed, bolted, shuttered,
We keep at bay the lawless streets;
Surrounded by our dear-won goods
The night is kept in vigilant view:
Our backyards, raked by security lamps,
Resemble search-lit Stalag compounds.

Far off, in another suburb,
A police siren wails -
Someone wasn't careful enough.

Untitled
Helen Murray

So far away, these are the best years of your life
And yet so near
Just one step over the edge
one bottle of pills

one bullet
one darkness to drown you,as you slip away
Like the people you knew, repelled by their own fate
And the poignant feeling of being watched
As they gradually realise
The seventh sense of sinners
Or how to play Russian Roulette on their own.

To Write A Poem
William Eagle

To write a poem, takes a lot,
For some it comes naturally,
And for some not.

I've finished the first verse,
But what do I do now,
And then there's the third verse,
Oh no; oh well!

Here we go then,
The next verse has come,
I can't think of anything,
I feel so dumb.

Fourth and last,
But definitely not least,
Oh well, might as well make the most of it,
And this poem.......is complete.

Roses In Bloom
Lorna Tait

The roses are all blooming fresh
The buds are glistening here and everywhere
They are like forget-me-nots
The golden fresh reluctant smell
The scent is filling the air
The colours are everywhere
For the pollen the bees buzz
The trembling petals are blowing
The prickly green spikes on the stem
The swaying sepals everywhere.

Rags And Bones
Margaret A Hall

All that he owns
are these few rags
that cling to bones
and skin that sags.

Too numb to think
or wonder on the 'morrow,
hope long since gone -
too tired for sorrow.

Bundled in papers,
what's 'news' to him?
it mattered once,
the memory's dim.

Too old, too cold,
he has no part to play...
Where did he hear these words -
"Sufficient for the day".

Love Lost
Mary Goodchild

I loved you once, thought you were a shining star,
But shadows dimmed your brightness,
Showed me how you really are,
And though the years have vanished
somewhere beyond recall,
I get no comfort from the thought,
I knew you not at all.

Star Crossed
Sandra Horn

With you
One night
I saw
A shooting star
Nobody believed
What I had seen
With you
One night
I saw many things
Felt many things
Learnt many things
A shooting star
was no big deal

The Robin
H H Young

I see a robin sitting there
upon my spade he rests,
god bless the little robin
he does my garden best

I love to see him sitting
in between the flowers
god bless the little robin
I watch for hours and hours

And when I dig my garden
he comes up close to me
pecks at a worm,
then flies up to the tree

The robin is the gardeners friend
He rids the garden of pests
god bless the little robin
He deserves the very best

England
A Ford

A new day is dawning, a new day is here,
It's a bright sunny morning, with sky blue and clear
There's a gentle breeze blowing the leaves on the trees
Oh how I love England, on days such as these.

Far away I can hear, on this bright sunny morn
The bark of a dog, and the sound of a horn

Small birds are singing from hedges and trees
Oh; it's lovely in England, on days such as these.

There's the sweet scent of flowers and hum of the bees
No country could tempt me to forsake all of these
For springtime in England, just fills me with bliss
How I love dear old England, on a day such as this.

Stand Beside Me Daddy
Mavis Beckett

Where is Heaven, daddy?
Is Heaven in the sky?
Why did mummy leave me?
Why did mummy die?
Was I a bad girl, daddy?
Did I make mummy sad?
If mummy left me, daddy,
I must be very bad.
I loved my mummy, daddy.
Did mummy not love me?
I'll be a good girl, daddy -
As good as good can be.
Don't ever leave me daddy.
Don't go to Heaven or die.
Please stay beside me daddy.
Don't fly up to the sky.

A New World
E Wilkinson

Will you take this little babe?
And show it all that's free
The air we breathe
The stars at night,
The moon, the sun, the sea,
Will you teach it right from wrong
And how to live in peace
So all the world may live as one
And its wonders never cease.
In return you will hear
The laughter and the joy
Of all the people on the earth
Woman, man, girl or boy.
There never would be talk of war
Or killing for the fun
Just a beautiful, peaceful world
In which to fall asleep
When our day is done.

Summer Love Song To Pale Bodies
Stephen Hyde

The gods of sex shake the blue skies
and the beautiful boys
and the beautiful girls

of the Earth begin to peel off
their clothes:
no fucking around this time!

I've come to praise the
browning breasts of the Summer!
the bronzing chests of Summer!

Make free your whitey arses,
haired or unhaired,
your bellies or your ribs!

Become brown beneath
your pubic bush
(but mind it isn't red) -

bake your body in the voluptuous sun,
then dip it in the water to cool!
Meet the Summer head-on,

grab it by it's lithe & sexy waist,
take it home,
light candles,

sweet-talk it,
get it drunk,
then fuck it as the sky turns gently red!

Untitled
Dorothy Mellors

What is this drug called HRT
I thought that it would work for me
But I seem to have lost my bounce
I measure my energy ounce by ounce,
It stands for Hormone Replacement Therapy

I wish it would give me some energy
Still I live in hope that it isn't in vain,
To be more energetic is my aim,
Or I'll return to the doctor and moan of HRT
Soon after regaining youth or the original me.

Our Kingdom, Our Great World
June M Blackwood

We have a home in which to live,
We have a heart, with love to give,
We have a mind, our sense to use,
We have a world, which we abuse.

If we cannot live together
In solitude and peace
If we cannot stop the killing,
And make the fighting cease,

What do we have to offer,
The children of tomorrow?
Will all they have to live for,
Be poverty and squalor?

If you look around the whole world,
Tell me what you see,
You do not see a happy world,
Just sadness and misery.

Let's make this place a happy home
For all to laugh and sing,
God gave us life and nature
And every living thing.

So let us make peace
And live as one,
It won't take very long -
If everybody helps us,
We'll make our kingdom strong!

P.M.T. (Pardon My Tantrum)
Jackie Atkinson

It's that time of month, when nothing goes right,
My nerves are stretched, and my clothes feel tight!
They say it's just water - I'm not so sure
I think they mean they can't find a cure!

I feel so moody - keep out of my way
I drop another plate (that's my third today)
"Don't fuss around me", I tell my small boys
"Just go and play, but don't make any noise".

They don't need telling, they know I've turned
Into this big frightening monster - yes how they've
learned!
I'm a cold evil witch (my husband says worse)
No wonder they've called it a 'womans curse'

I've tried vitamin C and primrose oil,
Eaten six small meals, but my blood's still 'on the boil'
For three weeks out of four, I'm perfectly sane -
Then on the fourth week I'm a monster again.

There's one consolation, I'll reach the 'change of life'
And I'll just have hot flushes - won't that be nice?

Wall
Kenneth Roberts

It is not long ago at all,
That night when they did climb the wall
They hugged each other, punched the air,
At last unfettered from the bear,
With axes they abused the rock
No risk tonight they would be shot,

The honeymoon now had begun,
The nation once again was one,
But in this reunited nation
Existed rich & poor relation,
The poor man drove up in his trabby
To the rich man's side of Checkpoint Charlie.

But soon the light would turn to dark
As the poor side failed to make their mark,
As east went westward in their droves
And with their trabbies blocked the roads,
Bon voyage, to where it's sunny,
To find the land of ilk and money.

The spirit of 'being ein Berliner'
Diminished as the purse got thinner,
The rich man wished the poor away,
With his memories of that joyful day,
And as the mark began to fall
Those in the west said:-
'Can't we build another wall'?

Thoughts On Peace
John McLaughlan

"Peace in our time"! or so it would seem
Is it a fact - or perhaps just a dream.
Can countries exist, each offering a hand
Whilst people still fight in their own native land.

All over the world, there is trouble and strife
With undue regard, to the suffering of life
Hunger and hardship, the lot of the poor
When great wealthy nations could offer a cure.

If only all people - from near and afar
Would throw off their shackles, and reach for a star
The star of humanity - friendship - and love
A star with it's symbol - a shining white dove.

To reach for this ideal, we really must strive
"To give" not "to get", to keep people alive
"To love" not "to hate", this dream we must nurture
Before it's too late, to plan for the future.

Our Five Imps
Ronald Nicholson Bennett

Our children all are little imps
Each has an impish grin,
They're always up to mischief
With their hands in everything.

But we would never swap them
Even if we could.

Although some days to be quite honest
We really feel we could.

At night when they are weary
And in to bed they creep
Those imps change into angels
When they are fast asleep.
Our five have had a peaceful night
We hope they will lie in,
But wait, a crash, bang, wallop:
Oh no what is that din?
"Come on, get up" they're shouting
"The night has gone away,
It's time for us to dress now
And go outside to play."

The Big Question
Tim West

Who dwells within this fleshy frame?
Who lies entrapped by mortal name?
Once formless, free, split not by false divisions,
I now find myself to be a needle;
Guided round by groove of circumstance,
Propelled indeed by nothing but illusions
that I call decisions.

And wondrous mirage of them all;
The I that sees and hears and thinks and
knows the falsehood of its own existence.
Bitter sweet this irony!
I know in truth that I am not
and yet linger with unshakeable persistence.

To All The Self Opinionated People Of The World
Duncan Dlomo

My ideas may not change the world today,
My ideas may not change other peoples
ideas to mine, and make my ideas right for today

For tomorrow my ideas may change,
And my ideas which were right yesterday
will be wrong today.

But it is for me to accept other peoples
ideas and judgements, without judging.
For me to accept simply my own judgement
I could never accept the reality of a changing world.

Poppy Day
John Capp

Poppy's on black lapels blaze
Like remembrance flames
In November's grey streets.
Still wind
Still silence
Salute the poppy's of a past
That sprung in khaki fields
Wreaths of war shall weep
Among the fallen leaves.

In still streets
Winters hazy light flickers memories

Like a movie screen
Voices in the gunshots
Fields that knew the pain and held the blood
And the sky so dark in war's clouds
The fire burnt amber horizons.

Autumn Sunset
Joyce M Colton

Flame-hued skies reflect the glory
Of the dying sun,
Shadows creep and lengthen,
Day is almost done,
All is strangely still and silent,
Waiting as the light
Declines and dims before the darkness
Of the approaching night.

In silhouette the darkened trees
Reach upward to the sky,
Burdened with their dying life,
They softly sway and sigh,
The fading leaves of red and gold
Whisper as if in prayer
And the sound is borne upon the breeze
That chills the evening air.

"Finished, finished," it seems to say
As the golden, dim light dies,
The day is done, the silent world
Wrapped in darkness lies
Until the earth has turned again

And the new day has begun,
When morning skies reflect the glory
Of the rising sun.

The Topiarist
Elizabeth Hogg

There was a woman whose soul
Dwelt in the nineteen-sixties,
The time of here flowery youth.

After deflowering she turned to vegetables
Organically grown.

This, she picked up at the Garden Centre.

Her final creative act
Was the study of topiary:
For a consideration
She would clip you
The heads of the Beatles in yew.

Very realistic, they were.

But now she has left the district
And George Harrison's nose has lengthened
While Ringo Starr has a blackbird's nest
Where his brains should be.

As to the other two
Scorching in summer,
Icicles in winter
Have taken their toll.

The Foxes Prayer
Marjory McGoran

Why do fox hunters chase me
My heart beats so fast,
Tally Ho they cry, but
Why must I die, or
Have they forgotten
Gods' all-seeing eye.

Alone Again
Josie Hickens

The days I can cope with
I keep occupied
The evenings they get me
Although I have tried

Watching the TV
Sitting alone
Self pity creeps in
And I start to moan

Why me I wonder?
Should I be alone
It's hard to be cheerful
I wait for the phone

Perhaps it will ring
Surely he'll call
No, it just sits there
All quiet, in the hall.

An Ode To My Mother
Anne Marie Diamond

They met in 1954
He used to walk her to her door
The romance blossomed, they fell in love
A perfect match from God above

Or so she thought, my mother did
A mother now with her baby kid
If the future she could have seen
I wonder, if I would ever have been

You see. My father he left us all alone
Adultery, my mother could not condone
There were three of us now, and soon to be another
Number four was my little brother

She struggled and fought through all those years
Too much sorrow and lots of tears
But through it all she raised us well
I am my mothers daughter. Can't you tell?

I'm very proud of my mother now
She should stand on stage and take a bow
It wasn't easy with two sisters and a brother
But, we grew up with a wonderful mother.

Purple Heather
Cyril Carter

Have you seen the bonnie heather
When it blooms upon the brae
Best in sunny weather
Or at the closing of the day.
If you've seen its shimmering beauty
In the sun's reflected light,
Then you've seen a part of My Land
That should fill you with delight.
I must pick a bunch of heather
Tak' it with me roond the warld,
To remind me of that wee hoose
Where we danced and bagpipes skirled.
When my travelling days are over
An' my banes are laid to rest,
Place that bunch of faded heather
On a once warm scottish breast.
If I should get to heaven?
Let me roam amang the heather
And see its beauty, tipped with dew.

Child's Eye View
M Banfield

Once I talked to children at play
And said "I'd like to know you all.
Which of you is Mary,
And which of you is Paul?"

"I am Susan, I will tell you -

My best friend is Clare.
She has on her blue dress
And a ribbon in her hair.
Mary has the red dress,
And Paul is very tall
And that is Richard over there
Leaning on the wall.
Janet has her cardigan
Buttoned up all wrong
And Michael is the naughty one
Sticking out his tongue."

One of them was handicapped,
Not all of them were white
But I was the one who noticed that,
They were just friends in Susan's sight.

That Day...
Maura McCarron

The day was a November Sea
that was hungrily, stonily, depressing grumbling.
I was a lonely clifftop sulking unhappily
The waves of sombre people buffeted me,
Paying their respects, yet wearing me away.
My granny died that day.

The day was a March River
that was lively; happily, excitedly tumbling.
I was a reed by the waters' edge, dancing in tune
To the river music, the birdsong, the sound of spring
Nothing could take my happiness away,
My baby brother was born that day.

The day was a July Rose-bush
that was velvety, beautifully, radiantly blooming.
I was a bud beside a rose, waiting
For time to dress me in splendour like she.
Yes, I hoped that love would have come my way,
My sister was married that day.

The day was a September Tree
that was silently, sneakily, mercilessly depriving.
I was a leaf on a branch on the tree,
Resplendent in my autumn colours, so I thought.
Unaware my life was slowly being taken away.
I found out I had cancer that day.

Wedding Day
S Hales

Today we've come together
In a celebration of life
To see two people we love so much
Start out as Man and Wife.

The bands of gold you'll wear today
Are a symbol of your love
And other things that mean so much
Like a kiss, a smile, a touch.

Today is just the beginning
Of a life that's built for two
And we want to say how happy we are
To be here to share it with you.

May the memories of your Wedding Day
Stay with you forever
And we wish you the best of every thing
As you start your lives together.

Redeemable
R D Allin

Passing a christian book shop
Many years on from a dog that has had its day
My vision transfixed by an enlightened window display
Typed boldly in red and white
The proclamation challenged my sight
"Look around we are lifting the veil, everything
half price in our Closing Down Sale"
Deep inside I heard my soul cry
"Has the word failed, find out before you die"
From this confusion my conscience gave a tweak
If redemption could be bought on the cheap
Take it on credit, pay by the week
I may need an ace
When he summons the lost sheep.

Understand
Michael Bateman

He couldn't explain no,
In the way we say yes,
To a boy who calls Mother,
The way a man cries wolf,

I couldn't explain the question,
That was put to me by you,
In a night of many colours,
In the colours, the night of blue,

All who said he falsified,
All who said he was wrong,
Should not pass judgement,
On the road that showed; how long,

And she said all in silent guilt,
Don't let them know we are as one,
Don't help them 'till they understand,

In one, as in two,
To escape.

To My Daughter
Molly Russell

The debt is now called in;
I understood even at your birth
You were not meant for my dear owning,
But just to have in short-term loaning.

How fast has gone the time;
Eighteen years is too small a span
To hoard the joys of your bright being
'Gainst the time of my rememb'ring.

Payment is your absence;
Your tidy room screams its silence,

Though on the air I hear your singing
And know, how hard is this repaying.

Renew, then, the mortgage;
You will return, from time to time;
Then I shall pay, with all my loving,
The interest due on all my owing.

Learning
Nina Cole

From a child to woman transition is brief,
a journey where hazards prevail.
The playground now life, is embittered with strife,
where the purity of heart is impaled.

From the cradle she wonders to crayons and books,
through the fountain of wisdom she bathes
Yet transition of youth is invariably truth
from the pathway of innocence she strays

From parental embraces she struggles to flee,
to seek independence her goal,
Virginity tarried, a weight to be carried,
an assemblage of youth that is soul.

From maiden to woman the act is complete,
and so then the frailty of years,
Like petals in bud, she feels wonder and love,
and clings to the remnants of tears.

From woman to mother the journey is fraught
A task to complete on her own,

He waves her good-bye and the we becomes I,
and she turns to the direction of home.

From child to woman transition is brief,
it's the process of living you see,
For life is a stage that is altered by age,
a constant struggle to be free.

Mothers Day
James A Whalley

Another anniversary
And other sons and daughters
Take to cars and trains
To journey for remembrance' sake

You who can no longer see
Or sense the tributes and the flowers
Whose time no more is counted out
In days or hours, how can we reach you
Greet you with those words of love
And hold you as we did
On such another day?

Grant me one moment out of time
To treasure - and in this place
A meeting and embrace.
No words, no tears
For thankfulness and joy will mark
The insignificance of years.

The Hurt
Janice Aslett

The hurt that I have suffered has yet to be concluded
I need to know the hurt, to feel the pain
To be complete, to finish off this game of life.
I need to know the pain that was taken away from me,
To feel the ebb and flow of life and death.

To learn to live and love life again.
I can hear the mans melancholic voice,
Who became, for an instance an intrinsic part of me.
The lesson yet hard has to be learnt.
The path I am travelling is strewn with distrust.

To give up and stop would be a manifestation of a
glorious dawn.
His toxic waste within me bombarding my head.
I am not his descendant, he must be eradicated.
His transference from bad to good is the mystery
unveiled to me.
My motivator has taught me well, to be my own
inquisitor.

To encompass myself within, to consecrate my feelings
Against my predetermined infantile self.
Be proficient in what I do, tread with circumspection
Along the way, to find to what I am akin.
Tell me there's no reason to suffer as I do
Is this my castigation to dwell with me forever.

Ode To Winter
H J W Dolling

I hate the winter days ahead,
Bringing their cold and rain.
The time of year I always dread,
And wish for summer again.

Dark clouds gather full of rain,
The cold winds chill my bones.
Deep puddles laying in the lane,
I wonder where the summer's gone?

Flakes of snow lay in the verges,
Where a robin sings his song.
Searching where the hedgerow merges,
Wondering where his summer's gone?

Darkness closes round my feet,
I shiver anew and scurry along,
To reach the shelter of my street,
And wonder where my summer's gone?

Raindrops beat on the window pane,
Outside, is a world all grey.
Indoors, I ponder once again,
Why can't summer come today?

Andrew
Nadia Cooke

A perfect house it used to be
with just my husband, dog and me.

Not a thing was out of place
chaos and clutter, not a trace.
But all that changed some time ago,
a little boy that we now know,
thinks ornaments are children's toys
and grown up things are made for boys.

A battle of wills it's come to be
with "Stop that now it's time for Tea"
and "Put that back for Mummy please",
"Let go of her tail" and "please don't tease".
Cupboards and drawers must spill their treasure.
Climbing the stairs is a pastime of leisure.
"Please get down or you will fall!",
it doesn't seem to work at all.

The only words he thinks I know
are "Don't do that" and "Andrew NO!".
Oh such a dear little boy is he,
say friends admiringly to me.
He gives a smile that looks so coy,
Our precious darling little boy.
A Perfect House it used to be
Who'd change it now, NOT ME!

To The Sunset
Donald Murray

Amidst the boulders, black and ashen grey
Lie many quiet seas of plenty; rippled now,
As the Kraken takes our Neptune for his prey.
And all whose hair in amber caught, shall bow

Afore the mighty beast of Norway's loins.
Adrift of truth, amidst the glare of heat,
They shall be seen: these sailor's coins,
That pay the way for brightest Crete

To sink beneath the world tonight in glee.
The shadow cast on all the temples bright
Shall not be found, there being nought to see,
Save stars in the wake of the mist. Falling from sight,
This day hath drank its final breath;
And so the sea and sky, awash with blood meet death.

Equality
June Evans

I am sure that some men
Who take time to listen to my pen
Those who consider women the weaker sex
A statement that's renowned to vex
Me and many more.
It is equality we are asking for
If only men would think again
Tune into us and feel our pain
To care enough to see
Their lovers, mothers, wives set free
Instead of years of misery,
Trapped, undervalued, suppressed
Told by men that they know best,
Why don't they give their voice a rest
And learn to listen not to test
Our endurance, patience, strength and love,
It's time for us women to be above

To take the lead, to speed
The case of womens recognition and position
Certainly, at least of equal, and in my sequel
You will see the weaker sex
Indeed no more, we are set free
A valid case of liberty
No more suppression, we will not be kept down
We will rise, some men will frown.

A Also Ran
Norma Fletcher

Since my life began
I have been a also ran

I never made the great school
I was the one who was last as a rule

My parents have wondered why
They should have, had a child such as I
The things I done made them sad
And all I wanted, was to make them glad.
But when I get to heaven's gate
I may have to stay a while and wait
As St. Peter peruses my life span
I will answer the best I can

There were many who made it to the top
The rest may be called a flop
For all who ran life fast, there's
Thoses who like me, can't help coming last.
But since the human race began
Where would it be without
The Also-Ran

The Realist
C A Bell Knight

At dusk I strolled along the path
when something seemed to clutch my arm.
As I turned sharply to see who was there
I seemed to sense someone trying to reach me -
but was only a low hanging branch of a tree.

Was that something I saw
flitting amongst the gathering shadows?
Merely a flight of imagination -
Yet I could have sworn I heard a sound
like someone in despair -
but when I peered closer - no-one was there,
'twas just a trick of the imagination!

I'm seeing things and hearing things,
my mind is playing me false;
It is only the wind soughing in the trees,
'though it sounded more like a sob
from a poor lost soul.

Discomfited I hurried along,
feeling a sense of unease,
thinking I was hearing a voice
as my footsteps rustled the leaves.

Alone at home, I fastened the door
to keep out - I know not what -
but did I lockout, or did I lock in
Something that tried in vain to reach me?
No! - 'tis merely my imagination.

Poem I
Len Harton

As one can see - poetry
Take it from me
Is never stationary
or just - stationery

The living word
Of our Lord
Removes bigotry
And insecurity
From the mind
Of Mankind
Who benefit - consequently.

To live - and to love
In His word from above
Is the epitome
Of simplicity

So come - study with me
Read, learn and take note
From this day you can quote
The rhyme of all time
"Be humble - be pure and live
In Christianity"

The Joy Of Youth
Joan Head

Can you remember, looking down the years,
When small boys laughed with pure, light-hearted glee?

Their sense of humour caught by word or deed.
Ah, yes, I know for many life meant tears,
Tears for the sadness in their hearts, and pain.
The loss of something which remained unknown.
Who never dared to smile and, smiling, learn
To treat fates stern rejections with disdain.
I yearn to hear that joyous sound again.

Where is there childhood now with simple joys,
Such as we knew in days when we were young,
Without a thought beyond our narrow world?
Then infancy was long and little boys -
The lucky ones, whose lives were trouble-free -
Grew slowly into teenagers and men.
Sheltered from worries of the adult world;
Blind to the sorrows of humanity.
Why should they cry for what they did not see?

Clubbing
Emma Phillips

Dolled up to the nines,
I interpret the signs
of the lusty, young and beautiful,
it's a flaming meat market
and *tonite*
I'm back on show.

Amongst the expensive beers
and over ambitious leers,
I feel like
the toilet floor.

Perfumed deodorised smoke
fills the communal air
as impressions are made,

I try not to care,

Natrel, Max Factor and me
are back
but
I wish I was hot and sweaty
with you.

Gone Are The Days
Arwel John Rowlands

Gone are the days we used to play
In our back yard, getting dirty.
Gone are the days we used to laugh
And tease each other - more's the pity.
Gone are the days, the lifetime of friendship,
In one single bullet, in one single shot.
All I have left are the memories to take with me.
Of the days we once had, that I haven't forgot.

Gone is the smile which once brightened the darkness.
Gone is the twinkle I once had in my eye.
Gone is my innocence and gone is my youth,
I am dead, I am dead, though I did not die!
My eyes - they are empty, devoid of all life.
And a look of anger covers my face.
I was young, now I'm old, due to horrors I've seen,
The horrific side of the Human Race.

Factory Of Death
Karl C Payne

Grey skies,
And freshly cut grass.
Remain motionless.
As another life story,
Is carried past.
Sobbing families
Wallowing in grief,
With messages of sympathy,
Written on every wreath.
People puffing nervously,
On their cigarettes.
A moment to reflect,
On happier moments,
And those of regrets.
They shuffle up the gravel,
As the Minister waits,
He looks so very caring,
Though he is running late.
He has three in the morning,
And three in the afternoon.
His brand new estate car,
Is parked in the gloom.
Favourite tunes are played,
In respect for the dead,
Then for the final shuffle.
As the curtain closes,
And final tears are shed.

Joe, Joe
Rosemary Skeates

Joe, Joe. How I miss you so
Even though it is a year ago.
Joe, Joe. How devoted you turned out to be,
Always happy and showing great loyalty.
Joe, Joe. Why were you a stray
You must have been a splendid cat in your day.
Joe, Joe. Why did we not meet before
I could have given you more and more.
Joe, Joe. In our home you enjoyed the peace,
Without the human shouts of "Get out, get out".
Joe, Joe. You were not granted long to live,
But you proved to us you wanted to give.
Joe, Joe. I am glad to say
That you managed to give us two years and a day.
Joe, Joe. What can I say.
Just, "You were the most beautiful ginger cat of the day".
We will never forget the love and the care,
That our little cat was granted to share.
Joe, Joe. In heaven there is nothing amiss,
Cruelty is an unknown word; there you are blessed with
bliss.
Joe, Joe I will meet you again. Till that day
I will dream of your soul, not far away.

Questions
Betty Jervis

In the strife-torn lands is there nowhere to hide?
Minds are narrow but the world is wide.
Between the wars a brooding silence

Erupting with chance acts of violence;
Excuses made and reasons given,
Man's hatred of man constantly proven.
This one is right - that one is wrong -
Where has all the tolerance gone?
Do we have to be regimented nation by nation -
Let's enjoy the variety of God's creation.
Is man so great that he must rule,
Can't he see he's just a fool?
Was all this set down when time began, or
Had God regretted creating man?

My Special Friend
Susan Groves

Friends like you are so hard to find
So warm, understanding and always so kind
Life seems to have hit you with such a hard blow
I've asked myself why? but I just don't know
I know you feel such pain and sorrow
But look forward, look onto tomorrow
You are a born fighter never give up or give in
I know you'll try your hardest to beat it to win
You shine out like the sun above
The kindness you give surrounded by love
In my thoughts you stay, think of when we are winning
As the sun rises and daylight appears
Remember with it, it brings a new beginning

The Blue Day
Douglas Jackson

I awakened on a summer's morn
To find an azure sky
Letting down a curtain haze
To tint the earth with blue.

Amid this dreamlike mystery
The trees but shadows were;
And streams no longer silver trilled
But sang in midnight shade.

Said I, said I, "T'will turn to gold,
But, oh, I uttered wrong;
Stayed it so till eve and night
Came with their indigo.

Lost Memories
C R Skelton

A wonderful thing are memories
One's clock that holds the past
To sit and gaze
Page after page
Till finally you see a face
No age

Innocent, so innocent
In a world so big
That brings to hand
To eye! It's all

To fill the mind of one so small

So much to see
So little we grasp
My childhood lost
It's gone! It's past

No memories I
Of child-hood days
So much! Too quick
It's all a daze!

Prelude
M Euanie Tippet

Some
Hold silence to be
The place of song -
The licence to behold
And to reflect.
We
But catch what we expect -
Yet this expectancy
Is in our blood and being brought
To some sure thought
Wrought
Taught
And set to flight
As glow-worm in the night
Seeks partner
By his light;
Thus are all partnerships

A partnership in full,
And absences
But folded wings.

How Many More Times
Jean Orrell

On Africa's hot and dusty plains,
To long denied life giving rains;
The starving children gather there,
Too weak to move they sit and stare,
Eyes filled with anguish and despair;
Their skins like ancient shrivelled leather
That scarce can hold their bones together.

I switch the set off guiltily,
I can't watch that and eat my tea;
The image lingers haunting me,
Of eyes that gaze so desperately,
And then I see through opened eyes,
Christ, crucified ten thousand times.

Life's Advice
Ron Wood

I'd like to live life my way
and find out wrong from right
not listen to advice
from everyone in sight.
It seems everyone's important
and tell you they know best

but they have their faults
just like all the rest.
There's often two different paths
that you can go down
I sometime's take the wrong one
and turn my life around.
Often when I'm dreaming
I realise life is real
and occasionally get these thoughts
that only I can feel.
I'd like to live life my way
whether I laugh or cry
and make my own decisions
before life passes me by.

The Pendulum Swings
Margaret Burrows

Smokey pollution hangs in the air,
Chimney stacks belching out everywhere,
Lamp lights so low, giving dimly lit streets,
Coppers with shoulder capes out on the beat,
Food shops all open to air, dust and flies,
Paper boys shouting their gabbled Street cries,
Those were the scenes a few decades ago,
Hygienic conditions, very low,
Running hot water a luxury, then,
Mod cons were only for rich gentlemen.

But females were not so afraid in the dark,
Or even to exercise dogs in the park,
The existence of crime has always been so,

But not to the extent we're getting to know,
What price culture in City and town?
Vandals are bringing our peace of mind down,
Changing standards, low morals rife,
Something's gone wrong with our way of life,
No respect for the law, or those who enforce it,
Burglary, fraud, we all can endorse it,

Who reared these toddlers that grew up to be thugs?
Sinking so low, getting caught up in drugs,
Who let them down, are we all to blame?
Will it ever rebate? It is such a shame.

Pain

A Rogers

I wake in the morning
My feet touch the floor
The joints they all scream
They can't stand anymore

My brain it tells me walk tall
You will forget
I open the curtains
The light shines within

Children play on the pavement
Their joints know no pain
I remember my childhood
I skipped in the rain

The sky above so blue
The clouds play together
Just like the children do

I watch and I wonder
What is pain when one has sight
Look to life's wonders
All will be right

Black Country As Ers Spoke
Norman Taylor

Owd Ali wos fedup a livin
he wus sick with a pairn in is yed.
on frittened to step airta bed like
just in cairse he drapped daarn jed.
sew he sent fer is missis ode Martha
ood wunce bin a right cumly wench
on er saw he'd slept wi is socks on
on accaarnt o the orrible stench.
Er stood theer un bawled aart at Eli
Yo know wots up wi yoor yed
yo'm askin fer trouble wi ye socks on
why do yer tak em off, like I sed.
If yo'n wore um a day yo'm wore em a wick
on they' stinking the ouse summat shockin
Yo cun just tak em off, on meck it right quick
on yo'll find that yer yed soon stops nockin.
So sure as er spoke Ali's yedairk just went
on e jumped aarta bed wi a shout
E chatted up Martha un borryed the rent
on went dairn tew the Pub fer a stout.

which just guster proove, if yo ai gorra bean
un cor raise the price of a drink
wer yer socks fer a wick, on yer Missus'l pay
if just to get rid o the stink

*The faint whirring sound you can hear
is probably Shakespeare reolving in his grave*

Written In Anger
Shirley Reed

Why is life full of giving
When little I get in return?
Why do I keep turning cheek after cheek
Whilst knowing I mostly get spurned?

Why do I try to be helpful?
So often my work is in vain.
I cannot keep check and stick out my neck
Again and again and again.

One day I will find a "like" person,
Who rather would give than receive
And I know they will want me to TAKE now and then -
Though I'll find it quite hard to believe.

Ballet Rejection
Jennifer Kilduff

Rejected and dejected at the age of sixteen
Not even an old has been, just a could have been.

From the age of five I've pointed my toes,
Stretched up tall from my heels to my nose.
Progressed to the bar, that's ballet, not drinks
G & T's later, at the other bar, me thinks.

Rejected and dejected just turned eighteen,
Still not even made it to an almost have been
All that work and a body that's limber,
Maybe I should go and start chopping timber.
My ports de bras smooth, my adagio's firm
And pirouettes on points, I didn't even squirm.

Rejected and dejected, on the scrap heap I'm tossed
Oh God I'm depressed and my confidence lost.
No more dying swan, no more handsome prince
Giselle and Odette I'll never dance.
I've had it with pink tights and point shoes
Tutu's, net and weight I must loose.

Rejected and dejected, but all is not lost
I walk with a grace and my head when I toss
Catches attention and confidence gained
So take heart, all young ballet dancers trained
Don't give up hope, we can't all reach the top
So enjoy an ice cream, and let somebody else,
In point shoes Hop. Hop...

The Wonder Of Creation
Marian Cooper Hilton

You lie in my arms now, light as a cloud:
Soft lips forever mouthing

76

An incomprehensible message.
Fingers, like honeysuckle petals
Curl around mine - captivating me...
And I can never tire of watching you.

Yet, as I carried you deep within myself
These past few months,
You were weighted... cumbersome...
So heavy in my distorted body
My legs could barely support us both -
And I quite resented you.

Now, gazing at my story-book hero in miniature,
I rejoice - yet feel humble - and so proud,
FOR I WAS THE VEHICLE OF A MIRACLE.

Pack Of Dreams
Ellen W Worthington

I saw him in the bric-a-brac shop,
A back-packed holiday boy,
Spinning dreams from ships in bottles,
Green glass floats, oily lanterns.
He had a nautical beard.

Later he stood at sunset
By a lonely hulk, long stranded,
Up to her waist in sand.
But the bleached deck and broken spars
Were alive in the magic light.

Chased by gulls under racing skies,
She was prow-thrusting in windy surge,
Decks awash round shouting crew, -
To the boy with the pack
Of dreams and a change of clothes.

Autumn Memory
N D Arch

I saw her scuffling through the leaves.
Cheeks glowing in the spicy autumn air,
And in my mind I was a child again,
Just for a moment I was running there.

Once more I saw the bonfires burning bright,
Thrilled to the fireworks flashing through the sky,
And felt again the chill cold breath of night,
Bring salty tears to childish wondering eyes.

Amused, I watch her as she writes her name
With chubby hand on misty window pane.
And watching, travelled backwards through the years,
Until I too was just a child again.

Autumn arrives to taunt us much too fast,
And Spring is soon left far too far behind,
But seeing life with fresh and open eyes,
Means youth and age are only in the mind.

Remember Today
Jacqueline Davies

Never look back at what might have been
Only go forward and find your dream.

Life is too short to waste time wishing
For things that have gone and cannot return.

Go on your way
Encounter each new day
With hope strength and courage
Endeavour to enjoy
Every minute of every hour
of every day

Remember it with joy
So of all your tomorrows
You can truly say
All your yesterdays
Began as lovely as today.

Time
Sheila Chalmers

I long to stroll slowly
In the sweet summer rain.
I need the time, I need the time
To stand and feel the pain.
The pain of time passing,
The pain of time passed.
I want to hold this moment
And forever make it last.

Time rushes through our seasons,
Time rushes through our years.
We try to find the reasons,
We try to hide our fears.
I'll ask not for the reason,
I'll ask not for the rhyme,
If God will only grant me
His precious gift-of-TIME.

Untitled
Georgina V Harris

Rapt in a tangled net of enchantment,
Silver and silver, blade or balm?
Bliss is the frantic dance of the catherine wheel,
Spasm the flames on a starless night.

Chess in the dawn of a changing morning;
When the sunshine has melted the light of the candle,
The moment has come; cannot linger, nostalgic,
For snow and smoke and enchantment to pass.

Dare in the light of the early morning
To abandon the comfort of the snug, tangled bed.
Be it truth, be it beauty or merely a shadow,
Don't long for it, turn to it; those lovers are gone.

Eyes newly naked must meet in this dawning:
Perhaps at the edge of a train station cafe...
But perhaps in a gallery of whitewash and oils,
Where birth may be born and beginnings begun.

Jungle Fervour
Joan Brown

I'd love to go on a safari
A real one - not nature reserve
To stalk all those lions and tigers
I'm certain I'd have enough nerve
There'd be a white hunter
Tall - handsome and bronzed
Who would gaze at me with desire
He'd tell me how beautiful I was
(And I'd forgive him for being a liar)
We'd trek through the jungle side by side
Exploring the wildest terrain
I'd pretend we were lost with no others around
He'd be 'Tarzan' and I would be 'Jane'
He would visit my tent in the dead of the night
And around me his strong arms would drape
But real life's not like that
I would wake up and find
I was just cuddled up to some 'ape'

Secret Admirer
Jackie Culley

For many weeks and countless days,
I have held you in my gaze,
I dare not tell you how I feel
All I know, this love for you is real.
So still I watch you as you walk,
We've never had the chance to talk.
I smiled once, I'm sure you saw,

These feelings are strong, I can't ignore.
I'm sure you don't know that I care,
Or know that you're under my secret glare.
But I'm your secret admirer, yes that's me
But I hide it, I won't let you see.
Because you might not feel the way I do
So I'll keep my secret love for you.

The Swans
V Khan

On the serene, gently flowing river
Under the slender, drooping branches of a willow tree
Glide a group of swans
Royal swans
Majestically they sail
Moved a measure by the slow swelling water.
As it ripples against their gleaning white feathers
Drops of spray sparkle and pebble their plumage
Ephemeral creatures
Long necks, white as the first falling snow-flake
Express their rare and wondrous beauty,
Their graceful flowing movement
Webbed feet propel them
Feet, grey-black, like the thunder clouds that roll above
Beaks, more yellow than the marsh marigold probe the
deep
Mouths, sift for delicacies of the uttermost depths
Or search through cool, luscious weeds
Which float there-on.

Neighbours
Fiona Ballantine

She fell out of bed,
cracked her head,
bled.
"She's drunk," they said.
Complacent and smug,
they shrug.
Compassion's a word
they've never heard.
You, Madam, and you, Sir,
would you prefer
to face judgment from above
on your sobriety or on your love?

Farewell To The Prodigal Son
Duncan Mitchell

Lock up your daughters in Old London Town
Cos my pal Alex is coming down.
He's landed a job in the big smoke
When the Londoners meet him, I reckon they'll choke!

He's going to the city to be a top diplomat
Yes, my pal Alex, he's thick and he's fat!
He likes a drink, does my pal Alex
After a few pints he talks like a dalek!

But we'll all miss him here in the Kingdom of Fife
And you never know, he might even make a cockney his
wife.

He'll be crossing the frog & toad to reach the apples &
pears
I hope he's not brown bread within a couple of years.

Is England's capital really ready for this man?
It wouldn't surprise me if he gets a life ban!
There's no doubt about it, he's a 'jock' through and
through
And he's off to London, I can't believe it's true.

He'll see all the sights from the Thames to West Ham
Greenwich Mean Time and the good old Queen Ma'am.
Och, well, he'll be leaving the noo -
Oh, my pal Alex - can I come too?

Screams
Katie Fuller

She came into a dim dark ward
Eyes filled with terror, nurses restraining her.
And then her scream rang shrill - "Oh God
Save my baby, they're burning him".

She clung to me shaking, sobbing, screaming,
"The flames are round him now" she cried.
"Get him out, get him out - my baby"
I held her tightly - "Hush dear you're alright".

Drug induced sleep followed fitfully,
Uncertain peace descended on us all.
Now and then she stirred and stirring whispered
"I must go to him - must go - hear him call".

Her nightmares eased, but she was silent
Of her one night of joy remembering this
That carelessly like throwing out her rubbish
One priceless gift was scraped into a dish.

Governed By Another
Steve Taylor

We give them natural warning signs
Yet still they never learn
Thunder storms and violent quakes
And now it is our turn.
They always lie for personal gain
Mans selfish greater needs
Broken promises lead to war
Hunger leads to greed.
The chances used time and again
A flaw in the human race
We're not sorry to see the end
The Governors of Space.
We are your superiors
It's time to say goodnight
The final curtain crashes down
The world has lost the fight.

Estranged Fathers
Kerri Moore

Detained to distance
In the knowing of your own soul.
Sojourn -

Instant identity - come find me.
Fathers of pestilence
Incessant.
You in my created entity
Possessed in line of honour
Remorsed for the sin of lover
Host upon host.
Creeping in, decay and stealing
Inches of subconscience
Sympathetic, the speciality
Of the desire to acquire
Handed and handled, twisted,
Brought to the attention of control
Aching for senses and identity.

The Day
Rachel C Chase

Sunlight fills a cloudy sky,
A ray of hope is shown,
Radiance beams from the face of the sun,
It glows and brings warmth to all life,
And dreams, like birds start to fly.

Reflections of light,
Are portrayed in a lake,
The mirror images of nature,
Beauty is revealed through creation,
It displays a likeness of the Creator,
For now only a glimpse,
Of that still to come.

A flicker of gladness,
Which bursts into song,
Something that cannot be restrained,
A tiny spark,
In itself a miracle,
When it is fanned into flame.

Through the fire comes healing,
Although at one time pain,
The heat refines and purifies,
To make something more precious,
Showing love in a fuller way,
What seems like loss is gain.

Ravings Of A Housewife
Rhona Bayliss

While gazing down into the bowl
At crockery beneath the foam,
I dream of how things might have been.
Of days gone by and ones not seen
I make up poems in my mind
Try to escape the daily grind
Housewifes chores and mothers tasks
Is there more to life? one asks.

A Helping Hand
W M Boorn

And I will gladly give to those in need of
Help along lifes lonely road

For if but once I shook my head and
Answered 'No' instead of 'Yes',
It could well be because of me,
That some poor soul with all hope gone
Would lose the will to carry on,
And so I'll freely give,
Kindly words to bring fresh hope,
Food to warm, and fare to ride,
To rest his tired and aching feet,
These mundane gifts, I will not miss
I have so much that I might give,
And but for the merest twist of fate,
It could be me
His lonely road, my destiny.

Pay The Dentist
Brigid McClathchey

Here am I
Face to sky
Looking at the ceiling
Dentist healing.
They used to be thorough
They used to be kind
Now it's just one thing in mind
Pound signs reflecting from his eyes
Listening to the muffled cries.
Not that tooth
That's o.k.
I came for oral hygiene today
Don't prod there
The pain had gone away

Now I'll have to stay
And pay
The pounds mount up
With the decay
Organise a follow up another day
Whip them out
Is what I say.

Castaway
S R Woodward

A foreshore ragged and unkept,
Flotsam tossed and rudely left
By the evening tide...
Night will fall and cast a cloud
On sea and shore, and every sound.
Though nature cannot hide.

Secrets and treasures of the sea
Spewed up in every shape so free
By every crested wave...
A broken oar, a spar, a crate,
Something lost by chance or fate
For scavenger to save.

On pebbled beach and golden sand
Wealth and waste lie near at hand
For every man to see...
The rolling tide will then reclaim
Things she left, just once again
On the coast by the restless sea.

The Cage
Lindy Elliott

Her foolish sisters wove flowers through
the net she was tangled in
and danced her to the ritual.

She bowed her head
and turned about her cage
to sweep its floor.

She turns again to seed her mind with patience
to begin her cloistered ministry of dust;
she defies the sly, bright madness of the moon.

Her powerful heart could storm
the naked fields of night,
her strong arms gather
harvests of desire.
But she turns about her cage
and locks its door.

Dutch Courage
Jennifer Allen

Just give me a drink so I don't have to think
of the horrors the day has in store.
I'll just have a drop then I promise to stop
and will not have a drink anymore.

I know I'm a slob, my monotonous job
has succeeded in making me so,

but life is so short - Oh, I've just had a thought,
I'll have one of those then I'll go!

Give me a break, you don't have to take
the pressures I have to endure.
I need a lift, the result will be swift
and I'll be in your debt evermore.

O.K. so it's wrong and it's taken so long
to erase thoughts from my memory
but it's different today, I'm in a bad way
and I need something stronger than tea!

Come With Me
Barnaby Jones

Follow me down the path of everlasting fun
Where people talk passionately below the rays of the sun
Rainbows shine brightly and the grass is always green
Come with me to this place and see what it seen
Frolic in the fields, cuddle together in a corner
This, a place of rest, where nothing's a tall order
Let yourself be free, celebrate your arrival,
Walk hand in hand with your never-ending survival.

Celebrate, communicate, feel the flowing rhythm,
When life first came to fill the void, music was given.
Sit and ponder on your fate, focus your blurred vision,
Happiness and purity is your only true religion.

Now that you're down that path of everlasting fun.
You'll soon find that soul-filling peace has only just begun,
Here you can stay for as long as you desire,
Soon you will be part of Heaven's harmonious choir.

Fantasize and fluctuate betwixt the real and false,
The dawning of your consciousness sets off a speedy pulse.
Everlasting love and catastrophic splendour
Can take you on this trip which you will always remember.

Wait for the good vibes, live in harmony,
Natural life is not new but you need it to be free.
Look all around you and see what you can see,
Feel yourself taken in by this one big happy family.

Children
P Rose

Lets our children show us the way,
And guide us in their innocent play,
Let them be our inspiration,
And rid us of this war struck nation.
Let them be our guiding light
And teach us to play, instead of fight,
If we all did live in heart of child,
We'd all be meek and all be mild,
So take a child as a model role,
Let their innocence touch your soul.
Protect our young, Oh! Lord we pray.
They're full of love, please keep them that way.

Re-Formal Landscape
J H Umfreville

Come forms, and legislate away
Courses for golf, where fat men play.
And paddocks, where pampered horses neigh
Preserved for leisure.

Restore the land, once green and pleasant,
Manicured for un-natural pheasant,
Plucked from the sky in bloody crescent
To Tesco's slab.

Frustrate that man with the double chin,
The planner with the oily grin,
Sure that he will always win
The ecu race.

Tumble fences on large estates
Electrified by potentates.
Close business schools for graduates
In Oriental robes.

Come, friendly forms, force open gates!
Prise footpaths from their wheaten states!
Restore fields from the declining fates!
For Metro pleasure.

Time
Josephine Harris

Time, the fastest traveller yet
With speed, the years it does devour
No transatlantic ship or jet
Can compete with passing hours

Time a span we all possess
From birth, to our demise
Some have plenty, some have less
Days go quickly, chasing by
To yesterday and tomorrows race

Time never stops forever running
Towards our future, come what may
Quick or slow, with endless cunning
Time takes us with it all the way

Mr Jones
Mark Whiteman

There he was behind each tree,
Pinning for the young and free.
Moaning on his harp he would play,
He would frighten all the girls away

Watching the sun upon their legs,
With whining strums he subtly begs.
that their eyes would die, beneath his spell
So that his hands could know them well

Some would answer his dark call
He was the piper and the fool.
Follow the tune wherever it goes,
and our stomachs turned like dynamoes

He said his music was his drug
He drowned in a bath which had no plug
His love song turned him to death,
He sang till he was out of breath.

We built a stable in his yard,
We pretend with our charade.
That we are him just for the day
and we frighten all the girls away.

Passion
Irene McKellar

Can passion be gleaned
After years of suppression
By a heart overflowing
With dormant obsession

Can a kiss rediscover
The vigour of youth
When with love it is sought
By a sensual mouth

Time is your enemy
The conflict well staged
Take hold and clutch tightly
True joy before age
Creeps in like a mist
In the silence of dawn
Experience the thrill
Before passion is gone.

Fix As Known
Tracy Lockhart

Your soul reaches into
Where I can't hide
Where you don't follow
I can see through
For what you are
And all that I am
To let your madness
Give fruit to my sane.

Memories Of Stourport On Severn
Lily Marsh

Just sitting
Reminiscing
Saturday outing
Children shouting
Sunshine showers
Halcyon hours
Riverside
Swans glide
Pleasure cruise
Deck chair snooze
Shady tree
Cups of tea
Picnic to share
Wasps, beware!
Paddling pool
Water cool
Ball games on grass
Hours quickly pass
Homeward singing
Memories lingering.

Untitled
M A Hodgson

These last few years before you're due to retire
Suddenly struck down before you've had a chance to acquire
All those things you'd hoped for through life
Since you created a family by taking a wife
The job you had came to an end

Much earlier than you did intend
Your back is bent you slouch around
Dragging your feet along the ground
It's not so bad as it was years ago
There was no social security then you know
Your father and mine survived those times
Raised large families hoping for better times
When things are bad and can't get much worse
Before the time comes to ride in that hearse
Count your blessings put a smile on your face
Accept your lot with kindness and grace
What to do, where to go
You hadn't thought it could be so
Nearing fifty it can't be much fun
But there's nothing to gain by looking glum.

Ask?
David Palmer

Why do I die in this world every day.
Why do I speak but have no say.
Why do I sing when nobody hears.
Why do I lie when I show no fears.
Why do I look when all is black.
Why do I breathe with this knife in my back.
Why do I mourn for all that is lost.
Why do I count when I know the cost.
Why do I take when so many need.
Why do I frown at those who show greed.
Why do I stand when I should be falling.
Why do I run and turn from my calling.
Why do I see when all you are blind.

Why do I hear in this silence I find.
Why do I fail when I should persist.
Why do I live when I shouldn't exist.

The House Next Door
Ann Slevin

It stands in the idle splendour, she lives alone within
every room is spotless, just like a brand new pin.
From each window hangs the finest lace,
every ornament sits perfectly in place.
The carpets made by Axminster,
the dearest you can buy,
yet, I wouldn't want to live there
and here's the reason why.

Gone is all the laughter,
just the clock ticks time away.
know one calls to visit
or to pass the time of day.
No tiny feet do patter,
across the kitchen floor,
for within those walls dwells grandeur,
where love once dwelt before.

Now she sits alone and ponders
on the time when life was tuff,
and of how she moaned the live long day
that she never had enough.
Yet, here she was with everything
that money it could buy,
she realised she had nothing
as a tear fell from her eye.

How Can We. How Can I?
Paul Ashton

How can we?
How can I, do nothing?

They say where there's a will there's a way.
Voices sharing reason pull and push the will of nations.
Helping unknown friends,
who share our dreams but not our fortunes.

Would any on the point of dying,
refuse the hand of any man.
So why when I sit fed and happy,
don't I care enough to share.

For those who sit and cry,
for food,
for peace,
for some little understanding.
Hands like mine come often too late.
Only with a smile,
a cup of tea,
a piece of cake.

Should I protest when I see wrong?
Write a letter, right a wrong.
If all would think as me.
What hope for them,
and what hope for me.

May I
David Shuck

May I, dare I
Yes, I must
Abandon fear
Seek out trust

May I, dare I
Nurture trust
Embrace with faith and hope, oh yes,
I must, I must.

May I, dare I
Welcome death
Seek life eternal
In every breath

I must, I must
Seek hope and faith
Through simple trust
Oh, yes, I simply must.

Soldier Boy
Robert Heslop

I've travelled over the world,
To places far and near,
I've done my service for my country,
And had my share of fear.

They sent me out to places,
Where no one ever knew,

I was in the British Army,
One of the chosen few.

I spent twelve years of my life,
Learning various skills,
They taught me how to clean my boots,
And do their marching drill.

They taught me all the things I know,
To make my life secure,
The twelve years in army life,
Were the best for sure.

My final day had to come,
For me to get demobbed,
And back to civvy street,
To find myself a job.

Charm
Gwynneth Curtis

At 20, his charm deftly farmed.
It oozed in swarmed crescendos
of buzzing motor-bikes, hiked
in loud macho-man heroics
on race tracks to catch the pretty girls'
fluttering eyes.

At 30, he charmed her innocence
to submission, farmed in advance
her charm with sunlight and sunset,
in his way and ways of men:

then the marriage bed -
love intended.

At 40, still that charm, but fed to others -
girls of younger years and coarse aged mothers
who shrieked at his obscenities -
harvested that charm, with memories -
charm darkened with a black moonset
that age incinerates.

By 50, that charm brittle - dry.
Old man's habits, old man's phlegm,
sour breath, belched wind, gobbed spit,
stagnant sediment, sweet sentiment - dead;
now only cynical love-making -
in his head.

He wonders at 60 plus, what was the fuss?

Children Of War
Marjorie Edgar

There is snow in Sarajevo
Searing sun in the Sudan
Children starving, dying daily
No one seems to give a damn.

Heads of Government sit talking
Wasting time as lives are lost
U.N. convoys stand abandoned
Deep within the holocaust.

Each one of us must search our hearts
For an answer to this madness
Each child deserves a better life
Not insanity and badness.

So my prayer for each young child of war
Is heartfelt, deep and clear
No more fighting, war and hunger
Only joy - and no more tears.

Walking To Work
Ronald King

Time was I walked to work each day.
Not far, about a mile.
Cats re-possessed the empty streets.
Once, a goldfinch on a garden wall.
On the busy slope, the distant hills
Lifted up my eyes, and challenging the cars,
I stretched my step, as if somehow I knew
The day might come, I wouldn't, couldn't.
Sometimes a figure, perhaps down from the hills,
Not walking as to work, would stop to speak,
Unanswered by the hastening crowd.
As she drew near, in long brown coat and battered hat,
I knew that she would stop, and turn to say,
"Excuse me. Do you think we live in troubled times?"
I'd smile, and agree that, "Yes we do."
And keep on walking by.

No longer working, walking,
I sit on my pension, and run time's video.

Freeze-frame the goldfinch,
The cats in different attitudes.
In these more troubled times,
When things just fall apart,
Re-run her question and my smiled response,
But stopped now, wait for her reply.

Heroes And Villains
Martyn Kendrick

All hail the stylish businessman,
his telegenic smile.
The carefully practised legerdemain
to hide the inner bile.

Women, power, wealth and fame,
all the trappings of success.
Cheating, hatred, hidden shame,
the trauma and the stress.

The chattering classes hero,
an Icon for our time.
A self-indulgent Nero
imperious to his crime.

The mansion, yacht and jet-set life
but still he lusts for more.
The pain and guilt, the inner strive
what is he looking for?

All mock the swindling businessman
his shady blood-shot eyes.

Expose his crooked masterplan
it's tangled web of lies.

Women, power, wealth, long gone,
these days a man of leisure.
Time to brood on what went wrong
and wait on H.M.'s pleasure.

Evidence
Bertha Snowman

Soil like granite
heaving to thaw
clusters of snowdrops
peep through cracks
pointed buds open
into dainty bells
flexibly yielding
to blustery showers.

Expanses of crocuses
capture the eye
massed together
profusely displaying
a blaze of colour
in sharp contrast
to gnarled trunks.
Rain stops abruptly.
Cold spring sunshine
kindles drenched hues
to sparkling brilliance.
Glistening raindrops

drip and vanish
in sudden gusts.

Winter retreats.
There is movement
growth, life, hope.

The Evening Bird
Martin Brazewell

Lone bird where do you fly?
Lazing over the water
Moving in slow rhythm
The sky is turned to gold
The day is ending on a balmy sea
How far is it you have flown.
Twilight is almost here
Night will soon descend
Hurry to your roost
Rest your weary wings.

Blue Love
Mary Smith

Dear Blue, now I see you

In the cornflower eyes of a Siamese cat,
In skies without clouds in the heat of high summer,
Or the icy blue air of a day in mid winter.

I know you are there

In seas without green,
The calm after storm,
The heart of a sapphire,
A haze of blue poppies.

You are within

Salomi's last veil, the colour of midnight,
The wail of a saxophone playing the blues,
A crooner's blue moon.

In distant perceptions of blue hills remembered
Dear Blue, how I love you.

Time
D Dale

If only time, that torturer of schemes
Could sometimes stop and give of its desire
A chance to hopeless unrequited dreams
Not only candlelight, but burning flames and fire

When memories are conjuring the past
And unachieved ambitions slowly fade
If only golden chances that would last
Had glistened to present their accolade

Time's unrelenting heart that ticks away
To fortify the monster it employs
Goes on and on to make each passing day
A cavalcade of hopes and fears and joys

Oh time, don't leave our yearning unfulfilled
Give of yourself for us to use you well
So small a span - our lives are quickly chilled.
How precious are the hours you dispel.

Me And Me... You And You
David Tallbot

I've found a kindred spirit
A hidden side not seen
Covered by a dark mask
If only.. just a dream.
You have a personality
Very close to mine
A problem with duality
I can see the signs.
I wish I could reconcile
This split within my soul
Just like me you're different
Two halves but not a whole.
I'd like to tell it all
But then again I won't
You see it's very hard for me
Please understand.. I don't.
So stay with us forever
Now we've found you there
We could really love you
All four of us could share.

Garden Hue
Leon R

The garden is a colourful place
We go out there with smiling face
For spring brings flowers with many a hue
Yes lots of colours red, white and blue.

First the snowdrop then bluebell
And yellow next the daffodil
And intermixed with these we find
Many other colours of a varied kind.

It's summer now with variety more
Mauve clematis one must adore
Then autumn comes with colourful berries
Most very small like miniature cherries.

Our friends the birds all chirp with glee
They're all for them and all are free
With flowers gone no berries to be seen
We're now just left with the evergreen.

Warning!!
Dean Homer

People arise in the morning,
Woken by the noise of a terrible warning,
Out of homes people come swarming,
Running, shouting, screaming, falling,
Injured men they start crawling,
Frightened children, alone and calling,

But no one listens to their cries,
When looking up you see fear in their eyes,
For clouds of dust cover the skies,
Thundering, growling, swirling, flowing,
At the centre, still a gentle glowing,
As nearby gusts stronger are growing,
Knocking down buildings, creative destruction,
Pulling apart with its powerful suction,
Destroying everything within a fraction.
Soon the earth is reduced to rubble,
Killing a land full of trouble,
Destroying the harsh, destroying the subtle,
A survivor looks up at the sky,
Clouds of dust still floating high,
Until there is nothing left to die.

Riseholm Villa
Norman Harrington

Attention is pulled aside
Low granite wall smarmed
By yet another coat of white.
Child's spade in bucket by the door
A gnome fishes in a plastic bowl
Windmill in a stick spins giddily
In the jostling carnival of annuals
Where the sun is made to shine.

Standard as sauce bottles
A tele flickers in the empty room
Stickers be-medal the window
Riseholm Villa is approved

By the whole world.
The face of the place
Pristine with make-up
Jazzes the eyes
The door stands aside
"Come inside darlin'
I'll give you a nice holiday."

Market Forces
Howard Baker

November, after clocks go back
And winter leaps forward baring its teeth
It is raining as I leave my office
And the wind is armed and dangerous.

No calls today, to add to the no calls yesterday.
No post except the wry farewell notes
From bankrupt clients, and job applications
From the dead who don't know enough to lie down.

The boarded shop fronts make the evening
Darker by more than just an hour.
The dripping placards record redundancies
Like wartime casualty figures.

I join the briefcase-clutching tide,
Channeling numbly into the bus station,
Brush curtly through the scruffy picket line
Proffering limp, damp copies of the Socialist Worker.

Their eyes have it, and it is called contempt.
All those in favour of apathy, say nothing!

You don't wanna read about the State you're in?
Kick the unacceptable arse of Capitalism?

Young and clueless. Success is recognising demand.
Providing the right product at the right price.
We could do business if you would only offer us
Grenades and assault rifles on easy terms.

Fruit Of The Boom
Leah Corper

Those pink shades of hell,
dazzle they peep out the shell.
When inquired
he was wired
his head took the shape of a mellow churchbell.

Does he have to explain, darling?
Why in his sleep, there is a snarling
but in the where
skins so fair
he shall arrive and seize your hand, darling.

And oh the men upstairs
trip over china ornaments
and ah the hangover over statues
to the left the ladies, to the right the gents.

Surrounded by the graceful ones
the women in their tilted hats
they can comfort with constraint
watch how fast conscience runs.

Daughter
Gary Booth

I am the stem, you are my flower
My finest hour
The sun does shine, you are twice as bright
Flittering butterfly in mid flight
My tear, my smile, my fear awhile

Golden swirls wild and free
Goes and hurls pretty at me

Daisy unknowing being desired
Always growing looking as wild

As the roots of trees, searching, looking for more
Inquisitive leaves gaily adventure to the floor

I look and see my past
And wonder what you would do
If you learned it doesn't last

You are me I hope I am in a part of you
If only you knew

Wonder
Dennis Sheldon

I wonder, when the world began
If things were where they meant to be
The same as they are 'today'
For the animals and me.

Trees and flowers, birds and bees
Make our country side.
Animals of every kind
In our woodlands hide.

Away from all the busy life
Our little creatures shy.
Oh it makes me wonder
It makes me wonder 'Why?'

Have things always been the same
And animals so shy
Oh I often wonder
Yes, "I wonder why."

Sonnet To Autumn
Eileen Jackman

The suns warmth weakens as the cold winds strengthen
While swallows migrate southwards again,
But robins singing cheerfully remain
As day light lessens and dark nights lengthen,
Tree and hedgerow leaves from summers' green turn
To shades of yellow, orange, red and brown,
And float silently to earth, or are wind blown
Into heaps to rot or slowly burn.
Sun ripened fruit is stored or cider pressed
As golden stubble lies in harvested fields,
And squirrels gather food the oak tree yields
Ere winter is nigh and wild creatures rest,
Autumn's beauty may fade but in natures seed
Eternal life is by God's hand decreed.

Mother, Daughter Love
Rosemary O'Neil

Daffodils dance in the wind
The sky has turned blue,
The world has come alive
Except for me and you.
For God has taken you away,
With you goes part of me too
And I am left to grieve
As only a daughter can do.

If one wish I could make
It would be for one last hug,
To share for a short while
That mother, daughter love.
To tell you that I love you
And thank you for all you've done,
To let you know I'll miss you,
Miss the laughter and the fun.

I'm glad you'll no longer suffer,
But my selfishness wants you here,
To have you as I've always had,
Through the laughter and the tears.
But now it's time to say goodbye,
My heart feels it's breaking in two.
Your spirit will stay with me always
Mum, I promise I'll never forget you.

Eyam Church
D Manton

Eyam village Derbyshire.
13th Century St. Lawrence suffered the plague 1665.
The vicar Rev. Mompesson organised villagers so that
the plague wasn't passed on.

Taking in the rural scene
The lovely church of Eyam,
The mellow stone the celtic cross
No hint of a terrible loss,
Its' place in history assured
The plague it endured,
Sacrifice, bravery, dedication
An example to the nation,
The Rev. Mompesson, man of strength
Contained the pestilence, at great length,
A true shepherd of his sheep
The mentor in the hour of need,
The events of years ago
Visitors passing to and fro,
Only stones now tell the story
The sacrifice the glory,
Yes church of Eyam
Surviving all the history it's seen,
You will still carry on
When we have gone.

That Tormented Heart
June Archer

How can you define the pain in someone's heart
The deep felt agony that tears you apart

The death of a loved one who e're it maybe
Someone close in your family
Mother, Father, Daughter or Son
Doesn't make it better - the pain goes on
Your thoughts each day are for them alone
The empty house when you reach home
Those little things you sometimes said
The cross words run around your head
If only I'd known life was going to be short
Those awful words we wouldn't retort -
But love - sweet love is always around
Peace in your heart will be found
You didn't know their life was soon to fly
How did you know they were going to die
No one knows - but you alone
The heavy heart - just like a stone
But don't be sad they're happy up there
Your laughter and sadness they will share
They'll look into your heart and goodness will see
But the person in torment - is Me!!!

Guy Fawkes
Bel Weldon

Guy Fawkes, I am told, was a little bit dim.
And one day Chalkie, (his mate), said to him
"Guy.. me olde pal.. if excitement thee seek,
I've a job for thee in parliament next week."
So.. Guy told his mum all about his new job,
And how he might give her a few extra bob.
Now.. Guy's dear olde mum, a lady named Fleur,
Was courting the chappie who worked on the door.

And.. Fleur.. (always being a bit of a snob),
Told her boyfriend ALL about her lads new job.
Always knew he'd get on.. a good boy is Guy,
"It's amazing what you can do if you try".
So.. that is apparently how the gunpowder plot,
Got nipped in the bud, by
Guy Fawkes... THE CLOT.

The Greener Way
C Bryony Mayborn

Oh, who are the culprits who destroy Mother Earth?
And who are the ones who can't see what she's worth?
Is it you? Is it I? Are we causing her pain?
Could we stop all those deeds that do make her life wane?

On No, 'tis not I, we oft hear you say
Because I do know what a high cost she'd pay
And I am a teacher who toils through the day
Instructing all others in the greener way.

And I drive to work in a great big green car
Most days buy my lunch from the Top Health food bar
All wrapped in plastic with a label that says
'With us eat you way into healthier days'

And when I'm at home I keep up the fight
Burning down trees that block out the light
Opening windows to keep the air clear
Despite my gas bill going up year y year.

And when I am cleaning I do what I should
Avoid nasty chemicals - use those that smell good
And I never use sprays more than ten times a day
And I'd recycle glass if I thought it would pay.

So. I think as you'll see, I do my bit
And the lax ways of others make me feel I could spit
But I'll keep up my good work till others do see
That the way to be greener, is to all live like me.

Confetti Blossoms
Peter A J Eariss

Cherry blossoms falling down
like confetti
when spring is married
to summer.
Falling on the heads of
young lovers;
a promise of a wedding
to come.
Or maybe a reminder
for old folk
when they too, were young.
and life seemed like
cherry blossoms all pink;
like champagne.
In ancient graveyards
the wind blows the blossoms
among the tombs.
Perhaps it is the confetti
used at the wedding of
our immortality...

Tears Of A Boy
Bernadette Morris

Here's a boy with wild dark hair,
deep brown eyes that angry stare,
holding back the tears.

Little hero, you don't need
to grow with such alarming speed,
holding back the tears.

Life is hard for little boys,
taking all their simple joys,
giving back the tears.

You've been crying in your sleep,
only then the time to weep,
letting go the tears.

You'll never be a child again,
soon enough you'll be a man
and you won't need the tears.

I will help you all I can
in your race to be a man.
I'll wipe away the tears.

But just remember when I'm gone -
heroes always soldier on.
They don't need no tears.

Feed The Birds
O Korbutt

With claws that cling to peanuts swing
And searching beak to break,
Hunger and eagerness to feed
Their clever antics make.

Like a mountain climbers every limb,
Is taking of the strain
Articulate power in every tendon
Nothing wasted all for gain.

Whilst beady eyes are bearing forth
Upon their fruitful fillings
Feathers plumped for from the north
The bitter wind is chilling.

Clutchin' At Cliches
Peter Corne

I talk in cliches' or I've nothing to say,
I'm cliche' ridden but it makes my day,
I bring out a cliche' for every event
Without a cliche' my vocabulary's spent,
The weather is reason for cliches' galore,
And then when it changes I've always one more,
They come out on Politics, babies and sex,
Unemployment, marriage and even my ex,
Perhaps it's cliches' that drove him away,
Whatever it was I had my say,
Always bound up in cliches' of course,

My stock of cliches' gets better not worse.
I can think of a cliche' to suit everyone's needs,
From heroic oratory to the latest foul deeds,
To cover all life's twists and turns,
And quote every author from Jonson to Burns,
How many cliches' do I quote every day?
Enough is enough my family would say,
Remember, too many cliches'
keep conversation at bay!

Newsboy - February Freeze
Hannah Piper

With outstretched arm he scooped and swept,
Each ledge and corner where the snow had set.

Whilst leaden legs did lift and rest,
And sink in snow so deep it tugged his boyish limbs.

But childlike still he played his round
With this white toy, so easy to pick up or push or strew.

A tiny human in a sea of white - none dared out but he,
On duty bound - to carry news to all who warm inside
Did wait to hear the stirring of the silence,
As paper found its way into the door.

Lone figure on a winter scene foot printing the white
Carpeted new day,
And moulding snow as potter would the clay.

Wood Love
Antony Taylor

Living, is something we only
do when together,
I fold up tight and cry all year,
keeping grasp a few thoughts,
wishing our eyes were blue.

I'm a small, hurt puppy, needing
to be picked up and laughed at.
Only four people understand me;
Only four! And I leave four-quarters
of them confused.

When I kiss you it seems our
toecaps meet.
And if this is special, it's only
tearing me; is this IT, that rare
squirrel?
Awake and lost, asleep (just), words
like 'Yes' stuck in my head.

The Search
Ben Fielding

I remember walking,
Can you picture me,
Plastic bag full of records,
Head still hurting from the night before the night before,
Couldn't walk,
Up to my ankles in could you spare and can you give,

Got home with empty pockets intact,
Looking for something locked inside a groove,
Haven't found it yet,
Trying to find the perfect vinyl fix,
To take me away from all of this.

Contrasts
Brenda Penney

Old Rufford Abbey -
Edwardian grandeur;
House parties and hunting,
The Saviles in splendour.

Society balls -
Royalty all present;
It's Doncaster races
And home to roast pheasant!

Our Rufford Abbey -
Well, really the Park;
We visit the Gift Shop -
We're home before dark.

Society changes -
Places live on;
Rufford is here
Through the Saviles are gone.

The Visit
Margaret Ward

Our day that was dull,
Our day that was drear,
Has burst into light
Now that Hayley is here.

Our useless chit-chat,
Our periods of gloom,
All have vanished away
Hayley's come in the room.

Just a few short months,
How time has flown -
We watch in delight
As Hayley stands on her own.

Our grey little lives
Are they really worthwhile?
Our answer lies here
In Hayley's sunniest smile.

The clouds gather again,
We switch the light on.
The darkness comes back
Now that Hayley has gone.

An Old Lady's Reflections
Doreen Jeffery

Yesterday was my birthday I'm now eighty two
The family came round for a bit of a do

The Grandchildren, I don't see so much
But they sometimes 'phone and keep in touch.

There were presents and cards and a big box of chocs
A thermal vest and woollen bedsocks
I don't go far now, perhaps to the shop
And when I return I feel fit to drop.

My husband died ten years ago
A gentle man and I loved him so.
We met at a dance when I was sixteen
Where have all the years gone in between.

And when I look over at his special chair
I close my eyes and imagine he's there.
I talk to him, telling him what people say
And how I've got through another long day.

There's one thing that really does drive me wild
It's the people who treat me just like a child.
I could never see myself being old
Sitting about and feeling the cold.

Our troubles were few and our blessings were great
Such happy memories that I can relate
And though I am frail I still have my pride
I'm old on the outside but still eighteen inside.

Passing Time
William F Burrows

My mind was full of young things,
Like ideas, and budding trees,

Ambition, new-turned land,
And enthusiasm;
Spring flowers and romance,
Swift urgency, impatience
For tomorrow, physical pursuits,
And eager plans
For future days.

My heart is full of old things,
Like dreams, and autumn suns,
Satisfaction, and harvest yield,
And contentment;
Sitting around with memories,
And nothing too physical; compromise,
The long years of loving companionship,
And fond remembrance
Of past, happy years.

Adopted Child
Sandy Green

Where are you now?
Sweet child of my body.
What part of me in you would allow my recognition?
What knowledge of me have you?
What thoughts about your coming?
Do you spare time to think of your beginnings?

Loved above all others
Swwet child of my body.
Perhaps you'll never know the torment I feel.
That terrible decision.

127

The agony of parting.
To give to you what I could never offer then.

If only we could turn back the clock
Sweet child of my body.
If we could only see how our future life would be.
If only I'd not made it,
That terrible decision.
For then, my child, your life would be with me.

Please don't ever hate me
Sweet child of my body.
Don't ever feel rejected by my handing you away.
I wanted all the world for you
The world I'd hardly tasted.
You'll understand. You're fifteen now,
The age I was that day.

Spirit Of Man
Robert Wlodarz

Cross the darkness
Salute the moon
Embrace the moment
Spirit is free
Time to go
Deep and far into woods of black
Be close to nature
Time will feel like an age
Purify and cleanse
As your indian spirit surfaces
Strip naked

Kneel and absorb
Evil is in the night
It will test you!
You will hear the voice
For this is the test
Respond and fulfil your mind
Experience emotions
Fill your lungs
And breathe your manhood!

Life Eternal
Suzanne N Bowen

Do not stand at my grave and weep
I am not dead but just asleep
I am the wind blowing in the trees
I am the sunshine on the autumn leaves.
You'll see me in the birds that fly
And in the clouds that go floating by.
You'll hear me as the rain does fall
And in the mornings as the blackbirds call.
You'll smell me in the flowers scent,
I was just a gift that God had lent.
So do not stand at my grave and cry
I'm still alive, I did not die.

The Viewers
Nicolette Thompson

They see on television.
Wartorn starvation.

Skeletal figures.
In sweltering distant countries.
The viewers themselves suffering.
From a diet of too much fat,
too much cholesterol.
The rain is pouring in England.
The viewers live in suburbs.
Catalogues adorn coffee tables.
Also magazines advising on money and career.
They plump up a cozy cushion,
watch the news.
Later turning the television off.
The cat meowing at the door.
They let the starving, purring cat in.
They feed it before they go to bed.

Where Once The Trees
Pat Ellwood

Where once the trees stood tall
And there were cows to see,
Now black tarmac and garages stand -

And in the fields
Where mice and rabbits once were found
Now stands a row of concrete shops.
All look alike -
Alive by day
But in the dead of night,
When doors are locked
And curtains pulled,

No longer friendly,
They are shuttering out the world.

When will the fields we loved
Completely disappear?
Where the sweet smell
Of grass and flowers
Filled the air -

Children as yet unborn
Will never know
The freedom we found there.

Summer Time
E M Fisher

I woke up early one morning in June
And heard the cuckoo calling its tune
I looked out of the window and not far away
I watched the golden corn beginning to sway

It was dancing in the summer breeze
Soon it would be cut and tied into sheaves
A flock of birds flew high into the sky
As the noise of the tractor came roaring by

Oh what a time we children had
As we took our teas out to share with dad
It was such fun to join him there
In the bright warm summer air

Dad showed us a mouse on an ear of corn
Now the poor thing looked lost and forlorn

A ride on the cart was such a joy
For every little girl or boy.

Crow Carrion
Lesley Sandham

I am a blot on the great copy book of life.
No, I'm not even a blot, I'm half a blot
Or a dot, yes, that's it!
I am a dot on the great copy book of life,
An insignificant squiggle biroed
on the corner of an old telephone directory.
A changeling child,
The runt of the litter,
An isignificant hair clipping on the salon floor.
I am the shame of Mother's Pride,
The ear of wheat that didn't make it.
I am crow carrion,
Meat for shiny black devils,
I am germ matter diluted
30,000 times.
I am a trap for men,
Claws and teeth outstretched.
I am evil.

I am also the Mother Earth
with tiny stars like diamonds in my hair.
I am goddess of my own existence,
Selfish queen of all I survey,
I eat a million of mankind
And throw the bones away.

A Room With A View
J Wallace Wight

Dear Old Town Hall
Standing so sad and forlorn
Seen from my window
Each passing morn
Passers-by often stop and stare
But nobody really seems to care!
A lovely old building
With nothing to adorn
Not even a flower bed or two
A disgrace to Kinghorn!
Let's all make a vow
Before it's too late
To do something now

Preserving a piece of history
And improving amenities too!
Surely is something worth trying to do!
Perhaps a museum?
Or some form of culture?
An idea that all could nurture!
A tourist attraction?
Bringing prosperity too!
Joy and pleasure to residents
In all that they do!

To the powers that be!
From a sad and caring pensioner.

Untitled
Alex Scott

When I went to the doctors,
His name was Doctor Chulse,
He put his fingers on my wrist and
Said I had no pulse.
He shouted through the speaker thing
"My my, oh my, oh my.
I think the chappie that's through 'ere,
I think he's going to die."
He said to me, "My chappie, have you got
One hundred pound?
Cause in a couple of days
You'll be buried in the ground."
I only went to see him, as I have
The chicken pox,
But now I know, in a week or so,
I'll be buried in a box.

Pepe
Ian Ferguson

With falling tears - we showered the earth
with grief;
Into the grave - his cover,
his toys,
his bone -!
company - for the newly departed carcass;

gone forever -
never forgotten...

REMEMBRANCE

A bush now grows -
above his nose;
the smell of death?
is sweet-!

Public School Love
Felicity Titley

Why do they think
cold showers
will temper boyish passions?
we know
that's just delusion;
showers are a sparkling
prelude to excitement
and,
on the coldest nights,
your rising fire
burns up the frost
and sets alight the dark.

Vision
M C Dowling

Oh beautiful lady with golden hair
Skin unblemished oh so fair
Eyes so blue warm when you smile
A slendour body, let me gaze for a while
You come into my dreams to my delight

Put your arms around me as I sleep at night,
When I awake you are there no more
Disappointed, I'm not, I am sure
For I know you won't take my world apart
As I love someone else who is close to my heart.

Abroad
Amanda J Cornish

Lying so close against you here,
Life seems so serene,
Your body beneath me feels like the beauty of Zeus,
My ear to heart beating,
My eyes to stars above so far,
The crash of waves hypnotise mind and body
through it's calmic sound,
And as I gaze at the pure azure blue,
the sky merges with the sea,
Creating a oneness,
And I find clear perception.
Small clouds relfect our sincere love,
And I wish that I could but glimpse the Emerald Flash,
To symbolise our love forever,
In this Bahamian pink land with it's conch lustre glow.
In this world I swam with sunlight spangled jelly fish,
Sheer reflections of creation,
And have felt the truth of warm dophin adulation,
But even these, compare not with my feelings for you.
This place has been a sensuous aphrodisiac,
Wetting my tingling taste buds as I watch the serene
yellow rising,
And feel full of hope.

Footprints
David Hancock

Two tracks of footprints, in wet sand,
led toward a tidal cove
where weed-wrapped rocks conceal a cave -
a sanctuary for love.

Racing the tide, footprints returned -
and other times were seen -
before the ocean washed that beach
as smooth as it had been.

A single trail, one misty morn,
led where that hazard lies
and strangely like a woman's sobs
seemed the hungry seagulls' cries.

No tracks returned, before the tide,
and none again were seen
after the sea had washed that beach
as smooth as it had been...

Lament On Peter's Haircut
Linda M Hinton

Gone are those copper tresses
That hung lock lustered from your noble crown.
Cursed be the blade
That severed your burnished strands,
Circumcising each tender tip of copper silk
For no mean eight day celebration

In Jewish Temple,
But for petty rule and regulation
In a jobless world.

Survival Of The Fittest
Angela Stenhouse

Life can sometimes be so confusing,
Priorities are often misplaced,
Which is more important, after all
Survival or face?

Peace after all is immortal,
the most important ingredient of life.
So why then do we have emotions,
to contradict this and lead us to fight?

Peace cannot be achieved by forgiveness alone,
The answer is not crystal clear;
Sometimes it never makes itself known.
Concern and compassion must be shown.

Life is too short to argue.
Gather your thoughts,
Face the problems,
Communicate.

An Old Oak Tree
C Brothers

In a field for all to see
Stands an old oak tree

For years we seen it grow
The branches used by many a crow.

It's girth has expanded by each decade
Too big now, to fall by axeman's blade
Through the leaves the wind will strain
Making a noise like heavy rain.

The spreading tree affords some shelter
In the summer when we all swelter
During the winter around it's base
Icy blasts the animals face.

Now when I'm old and grey
I hope that I still can say
In a field for all to see
Stands a very old oak tree.

Alice
O M Cribb

I gaze in wonder at the plight
of Alice, though without her sight
contentment full upon her face
her nimble fingers making lace.

How then could I? perhaps with equal grace,
but discontentment showing on my face,
create such intricate designs as she.
Yet I can see.

These gifts bestowed on Alice being blind
reflects a joyous heart and peaceful mind

a sense of touch, to use such gifts
she may possess, despite her plight
with inner sight.

The Christmas Alphabet
M S Craven

A are the angles good tidings did bring,
Bethlehem the birthplace of Jesus their king.
C is the carpenter, Joseph by name,
Deity celestial to his wife Mary came.
Exalted her highly, saying be not distressed,
Favoured of women, God thee has blessed.
Harken to me now on Christmas morn
In the city of David a boy child will be born.
Jesus the name is what you must choose,
King he will be over the Jews.
Loudly will the angels sing glory to this new born king.
M is the Manger, the holy babe's bed,
Nestled in hay in that lowly shed.
Over him Mary her vigil doth keep,
Patient the oxen in stalls asleep.
Quiet the world on this holy night,
Round the stable a star shines bright.
S for the stable, the shepherds, the star,
That guided some travelers who came from afar.
U is the unity at this time of year,
Valued the meetings with friends we hold dear.
W the wise men from countries afar,
Xpert their wisdom in following the star.
Y is for yuletide, best time on earth,
Zestful we celebrate the Christ child's birth.

The Great World War 1914-1918
Thomas Harvey

The whispers of death as you go over the top,
shell fragments and bullets whistling all day.
Why, we ask ourselves, why do they murder us?
Fight for your king and your country they say.

When we first enlisted with the army.
they said "You will live, you'll all be famous folks."
What terrible liars they were,
oh what a wicked joke.

The shelling had stopped, the whizz-bangs were silent,
the men were waiting for the dreaded whistle to go.
The whistle of fear, the whistle of murder,
they were waiting for their death wish to blow.

The whistle has blown several times,
the beginning of the end is near.
The men were running over 'no mans land'.
There was no going back now, though filled with fear.

I'm through the wire but with many cuts,
I'm on the way to the enemies trench.
The machine-guns have started with a pop popping noise.
My face is going terribly blench.

Quick men jump into their trench,
batter their brains out, stab them in the eye.
How can we do that sarge, they're only men like us.
shut up and kill them, make sure they die.

Retreat, retreat run like the wind.
The counter attack is starting up.
Keep running like a mad man, like the clappers,
don't look back to your death toll.

Valencian Evening
Elizabeth Hillman

The sky loses its brightness
And the small walled orchard
becomes a miniature forest
Where gleaming oranges and lemons
Are golden and yellow globes
Hung like lanterns to light
The dusk-creatures' prowlings.
Beyond the wall, upon the stony path,
Two horses pass, and murmured voices
Grow louder, then slowly fade;
The miller and his son, going to the inn,
Or weary knights coming from a far battle?

Country Boy
Mary Mycock

Sunny lazy days by the river
Splashing friends to a cold shiver
Through quiet leafy lanes by bike
Excitement, joy, flying a kite
Nut, bolts, screws, engine pieces
Trousers oily, full of creases
Sheep bleat, hens cluck, cows moo

Cats mew, dogs bark, birds coo
Your life on the farm
Ready to tell a good yarn
Boots heavy in the ground
Spade pushing soil to a mound
Grown from lad to young man
Helping people all you can
Driving tractors, wheels skidding
Rush, scurry, always hurrying
Lifes sixteen years full of chatter
Your dreams will soon shatter
Loudly ring the church bells
A tractor carved in marble tells
At peace in Gods loving arms
Forever praised with our psalms.

To my son Steven
born May 1976, died Sept 1992

Feathered Ballet
Malcolm Bucknall

Swooping - from the spacious heavens -
Gliding silently - in flight,
Peacefully - with gentle motions,
On rippled surface - gulls alight.
Their plumage glowing in the blue sky -
As they drift, with motions slow,
Whirling down to crested waters
On the dancing seas below.
Majestic in their regal splendour -
Their feathers soothed by tranquil breeze,
With elegant distinguished motions
They settle on the placid seas.

Magnificent Oak
Julie C Stoker

See you standing tall and proud
A wonderful sight to see
Like a gentle giant, branches bowed
You're a truly magnificent tree

You've stood for so long, centuries old
An eon since you were born
It's hard to believe that something so bold
Sprang forth from a timid acorn

My respect for you is truly immense
I'm completely in awe of you
Your beautiful leaves so green and dense
Promise hope and great strength anew

You hid a King within your green cloak
And his life you saved
We're proud to call you the Royal Oak
As our Heritage you have paved

You've been here for so very long
As timeless as eternity
So I know while you stand tall and strong
England will always be

Ballad Of The Giro Man
Eileen V McGough

Within his concrete flat he whiled away the hours.
He envied all the business men who lived in ivory towers.

He wanted things he'd never have, he wanted to belong.
He tried to curb his restlessness, he knew that he was wrong.

He queued up every fortnight and he signed a dotted line.
Wearing faded denims and the inner city grime.

When he got his meagre giro he lived life for a day.
Then in his concrete council flat he whiled the hours away.

He'd never owned single thing that people thought worthwhile.
He often thought his drab, grey life was dragging like a trial.

He'd given up the fruitless search for work of any kind.
He told himself that he was left with nothing else to find.

He didn't care about the things that happened in the world.
He tried to isolate himself and never spoke a word.

He dreamt he stole a motor car and drove it all the day.
Then in his concrete council flat he whiled the hours away.

He told himself that just for once he'd like to bid for fame.
Let people know that he had lived and even had a name.

He thought about his days at school, how little he had learned.
Of how he'd let his parents down and all that they had yearned.

He turned the television on and watched some quizzing games.
And wondered why he never would remember any names.

He felt a kind of hopelessness surround him where he lay.
Then in his concrete council flat he whiled the hours away.

Insomnia
E Barkley

In the dark reaches of the night
When all is quiet and I can't sleep
I listen to the house groan and creak
I hear the trains go thundering by
And listen to their mournful cry
I listen to the call of the midnight owl
And the screech of the ally cat on the prowl
The clock ticks on in a quiet room
And early morning light
Breaks the inky gloom
The sunrise heralds a new day dawning
And I fall asleep gently yawning!

Country Air
Sheila Dunn

The pride of the trees, the swiftness of streams,
The water rushes and shatters our dreams,
The hills are high, the grass is green
The rushing swift stream, is the dearest thing I've seen.

Maybe a bird will chatter and tweet.
Maybe the stream has hidden feet,
For it rushes and rushes, over rocks sand and shore,
It rushes and rushes through cracks, and curves
evermore.

When the trees are blown gently, by the winds so fair
I think of something that happened,

Maybe a year or two ago, I'm nearly over it now.
But I know I'll never forget, the country air.

Pot Pourri
Brenda Phillips

If every song thrush
joined in chorus
to sing a love song
just for you,
if every scented petal
could be crushed
into a pot pourri
to make you a pillow,
if every star could shine
to light your way,
if every vine
could give its wine
to fill your cup,
if you could hold
each soft new baby
in your arms,
you still would not
sense the pleasure
I would wish for you
nor know the joy
that loving you
has given me.

My Everyday
Mavis Stoker

Washing, cooking, cleaning, scrubbing
Another day dawns, the brass needs rubbing
Hanging curtains, polishing windows
A look at the clock, my! how the time goes

Out to the shops, there is food to buy
We keep on eating, why oh why?
Home again with tins, jars and a packet
I see I have lost a button from my jacket

Lunchtime comes as way of a treat
It gives me a time to rest my feet
Then washing up just has to be done
A chore I find that is not much fun

Hands covered in flour, a ring on the phone
Just let it ring, pretend I'm not home
Answer it now I know is best
To know who it is will put my mind at rest

The day advances, the family is home
No more time to spend alone
Evening meal finished, dishes put away
I wouldn't for the world change my Everyday

My Boys
T M Loach

Oh what joys,
A house full of boys,

Jumping and tumbling,
Do stop grumbling.
Think of the laughter,
That sounds ever after.
Long after their fed,
And tucked up in bed,
The moment you treasure,
Oh what a pleasure,
To sit without care,
In your favourite chair.
You're never stopping,
Forget the washing,
Have a moment or two,
You have but a few.
Its all part of raising,
And sometimes praising,
A house full of boys
But oh what joys.

Postnatal Depression
Joanne Lawrence

For me, it's not coping with the simplest of things,
Suffering terribly with the stress that life brings.
Knowing everything I lay my hands on goes wrong,
Needing someone to make my decisions to be strong.
Forgetting the important matters which is frustrating and sad,
Wondering each day, each attack, if I'm really mad.
Wondering whether to give in to it or fight,
The despair, the panic, the anger, it's not right,
I'm so scared I'll be like this forever,
Frightened that I'll be like this forever,
Frightened that my husband will leave, that we won't be
together,

I guess not being able to control myself at all,
When the depression creeps up and breaks down my defence
wall,
Sometimes shutting out my life, feeling full of reject and
scorn.
It all started two months after my baby was born
Fear, threw suicide tendencies out of the window,
But the feeling my life is pointless has now had chance to
grow.
Sometimes I feel determined to fight this thing to the end.
I think it would be easier to have a 24hr friend,
Somebody to take the stress I'm faced with away,
Deal with it accordingly, so my future is not so grey,
Someone to boost my confidence when I feel I could just die,
Someone to answer why is this dreadful nightmare happening
to me.
Why?

David
Sheryle Hammond

David was an ignorant lad,
He took no notice of his mum or dad.
Even when he was at school
to ignore everyone was his rule.
He marched in the classroom towards his chair,
Scruffy clothes, messy hair
The way he dressed was of no concern,
It seemed he would never learn.

Kids tried to talk to him, but all in vain,
he ignored them just the same.
He was always in a world of his own,
no attention to the teacher was ever shown

Homework was set, and next day completed,
but he sat in his chair and willfully repeated,
"The homework you set I did not do,
Simply because it was set by you!"

Lesson was over, children sat with relief,
waiting for teacher to say they could leave.
But David had already risen from his chair,
and walked out of the room without a care.
The teacher took no notice, and held her breath,
then very quietly dismissed the rest.

Mother
Lesley James

When we were together
We loved each other true
But now that you're not here with us
You've left us feeling blue
Our hearts are broke down deep inside
Oh will they ever mend
You weren't just our mother
You were our dear best friend.

We gave each other years gone by
Our memories to hold on
As soon as you did slip away
We felt that you had gone
Our hearts are broke down deep inside
Oh will they ever mend
You weren't just our mother
You were our dear best friend.

Amanda
Roger G Jackson

We have a little lady.
No more is she a baby.
She sings and shouts
And whistles too.
She is a darling, that is true.

Her eyes are green.
Her hair is sheen.
Her skin is like milk and honey.
Everyone says, I do believe,
She looks just like her mummy.

Her name is Amanda
So fine and strong,
A little girl, who in my eyes
Can do no wrong,
We love her now, as we shall always do
Her daddy, her mummy and Deena too.

Reply To An Invitation
Barbara Moore

Your multi-coloured patchwork coat
May catch the eye, my dear,
But, seen at closer quarters,
Its seams are raw, I fear.

I must ask, did you really hope
To dazzle or impress
With borrowed rags of Wendy Cope
To brighten up your dress?

All women love a bard, you say,
And that may well be true;
But words of wisdom, wit or rage,
Words that live on from age to age,
Words that come burning off the page
Eternally are new.

So, what about those borrowed lines?
A joke perhaps, to share?
An innocent deception?
Maybe, but I don't care.

Your poem's botched and cobbled,
Your own voice faint and thin -
Send it to some less literary girl,
Or put it in the bin.

The Old Man
Carol McGahey

He sat all alone on the seat
A bag of bread in his feeble hands
Calling the ducks who came
With loud quacks and waddling feet
The old man watched the boys go by

And thought of how they reminded him
Of two boys long ago
He closed his eyes and rubbed his chin
Ah! Yes himself and Tom
They had spent their summer days
With farmers working at the hay
There was no time for play
The one great joy was Bess the horse
Who pulled the cart along
They rode upon her back
When the longs days toll was done
A tear slipped from the old mans eye
When he thought about his chum
The war had parted them as men
But he would not forget the boy.

Untitled
Leonard Bromby

Black cape. Peaked hat.
Black magic. Black cat.
A black heart made of stone,
A black witch. Evil crone.

Eye of toad and hair of cat
Head of fish. Hair of bat.
A seething cauldron - An evil brew.
Wicked eyes of fiery blue.

A chicken's head complete with hackle
Dripping blood. An evil cackle.
Evil spells are in the making
Whilst in the oven a boy is baking!

Witches eat young girls and boys
And are given to using ploys,
To lure them into a cottages inner
Where they become a tasty dinner!

Beware, young children, do take care
Avoid the evil witch's lair.
Do not enter those woods so thick
Run back home to mother. Quick!

The Bride
Stephen Herbert

The bedroom was no more than a waiting room.
An ante chamber, holding the final door to marriage.
As soon as I step out I will drown
In the sea of a million smiles.

My father calls through the door, "Second thoughts?"
No it's my first!
He calls again "we're leaving."
I have left.
The jeans and T-shirt have now faded the nausea of the
dress,
As I sit across from the faded church
I see him pace nervously round the litchgates,
The sea of smiles lapping impatiently around his head.

As I drive past, I wave, I toot, I look through my mirror
I see him drown in a sea of open mouths.

I did not have second thoughts
It was my first!

Limbo
Donald Cameron

The mediocre man
fell down one day and died,
the poor old sod.
His well bred wife,
to whom he'd been a trial,
declared in spite of that
he'd gone to God.
But for the trail to paradise
his feet were poorly shod,
and couldn't cope with stepping
where the sheep had safely trod.
For all that though it's likely
he'll be equal with all others
in the limbo where he'll end up
on his tod.

Decree Absolute
M J Hore

You made me a house in a wood
Under a tree
You levelled the ground and laid a mat floor
Simply for me

The tree was a larch still green
In the needles of spring
We lay on our floor our heads on our arms
And heard the birds sing

We warmed up our hearth to flame
And watched it take fire
We baked there a batch of good bread to nourish
Our hearts desire

And when we woke in the mornings
We shared the same cup
You rose first then leaned down to kiss me
And cover me up

Then you left me to sweep and tidy
And make our home clean
And I took up the floor and the grass sprang again
Empty and green

And there never had been any house
And the hearth was cold
The bread was gone and the cup broken
And the story told

Deserted Cemetery At Barnes
A Pink

An angel with no head leads me in
to wander through tombstones
shrouded with ivy and brambles.

From cypress trees the doves repeat their call,
"Take two leaves Taffy, take
Two"? endless as the deaths below.

The heirs of Pax Britannia lie here.
Families who celebrated
the Empire's apogee.

How firm were their beliefs in God's rewards.
They went to meet their Maker sure
of joy in Heaven.

Many a young man fell in foreign climes.
"Died for his country, and his Queen",
a fitting epitaph.

Others at home. One, Thomas Arkwright,
"An upright man who toiled
on earth to win his Heaven".

Poor Sarah Brown went, "Happily to meet
her Lord, hoping for a rest
from earthly toil and pain".

I walk among these worthy ancestors,
eating the glossy blackberries
that grow from mouldering bones.

Were those that rest below me godly folk,
or were they simply, as we are
mistaken in their purpose?

It starts to rain. Big drops splash softly
on the living and the dead.
I turn for home, alone.

Tramp Cat
Eric Adams

Poor cat, you were but skin and bone
When first you came to grieve us,

And tired of living on your own;
Truffles, why did you leave us?

You crawled upon our laps and purred,
Heart open to receive us,
But crept out when the daylight blurred;
Truffles, why did you leave us?

We swore each one to be your friend,
Why could you not believe us?
We were your home and journey's end;
Truffles, why did you leave us?

Dear cat, we loved you like a child,
How could a child deceive us?
You were too weak, too proud, too wild
To live, and not to leave us.

The Gale
Alfred Matthews

The great tree, writhing, heaving
Branches bowing to the clouds,
Shedding leaves - its clothing
To furnish green shrouds
For hapless fledglings
Fallen from their nest.

They lay bare, forlorn,
Mouths agape, plumage matted,
No soft down - no mother's
Beak to preen them.
Cold, wretched, pathetic, unfed,
Not ready yet for flight.

Nature, their bodies she will use
The cycles to complete.
Roots absorb their substance,
Next year's leaves will protect
Another brood of nestlings.
Will they survive Nature's cull?

The Market Square
Gwen Mackay

Whilst sitting eating fish and chips
Outside the market square
Upon a wooden seat - a gang
Of lads I was aware
Dressed up in leather jackets
Dazzled by their get-up gear
The usual metal badges
An earring through each ear.

I stared in anxious wonder
As they talked of this and that
As inside one's crash helmet
Sat a fluffy tabby cat
Occasionally, with gentle hands
Each lad between odd bites
Would feed it tiny scraps of fish
Then went off for their bikes

It wasn't long before the roar
Of engines raced on by
And cuddled up inside his coat
The kitten caught my eye
Its little face with great blue eyes
Without a sign of fright

I swear it grinned as they roared off
Into the warm sunlight.

Birds (I)
Thomas F Carroll

Flint made a 'mint', the 'birds' were not 'skint'.
The chevy and the caddy were a symbol of the gravy.
As the cars ounced bounced along the assembly line.
The town sang chirpy as the bread rained down.

Here I am in Flint - America's poorest town
The blackbird's song of poverty chills the sheriff's ears.
The homeless chicks eyes are full of tears.
The hawk appeared with his evil eye
and carried the nest-egg to a distant land.

The robins are crying come back golden goose -
as the vultures bide their time.
The flamingo asks where is the hawk?
The owl hoots Mexico - the crow squawks why?
To pay the sparrow seventy cents an hour
was the curt reply.

The eagle and the bullfinch both agree
that the hawk is free to devour its prey.

Leaflet Distributing
Shirley H Ford

Leaflet distributing is a job you should not chose
Unless you have upon your feet a pair of cumfy shoes.
You also need a shoulder bag to carry all your stuff
And then a sense of humour for when the job gets tough.

You require a sense of purpose to keep up a steady pace
And also of direction to ensure return to base.
It helps if you possess a map with street names written in
And don't despair if people put your leaflets in the bin.

You should always carry plasters for blisters on your toes
And for your wounded fingers on which letter-boxes close.
Old folk will want to chat with you but you just haven't time,
You have a lot of paths to walk and many steps to climb.

You will no doubt meet the Baker and other Tradesmen too
And Canvassers and Salesmen, all rushing round like you!
Sometimes you'll find they all converge upon the self-same
door
And then you have to nip in quick, your leaflet to the fore!

But life will have its brighter side when weather's all set fair,
For birds will sing and flowers will waft their perfumes in the
air.
You'll find amusing notices pinned up on some folks' door
And then you'll think your job is fun instead of just a chore.

Yes, Leaflet Distributing, when all is said and done,
With the right equipment has no comparison,
For some folk will be pleased to get your leaflet through their
door
And if your Boss is satisfied he'll send you out with more!

For My Sons
J Green

When I was little, once, I too,
Gathered flowers for my mother, just like you,
Wondered over the spider's web
Bedecked with diamonds, just as you said.
Exulted over the rain on my face
When I was a child and full of grace.

Stay little, my sons, for when you grow,
All wonders fade, most ideals go.
We have so short a time for play
Soon we grow up and grow away
With broken dreams and lost illusion,
Left behind in sad profusion.

So be babies yet for a little while,
Together we'll play, and love, and smile,
Too soon you'll be men, and away you'll grow
And I shall have to let you go.
May your lives be happy and full of joys
But don't lose your dreams too soon, my boys.

Oh, for the days of childhood,
Laughing, happy and gay.
Where are those days of the past now?
Gone forever away!

Love Suzanne
L Clark

Love is like the sun,
Shines so bright then turns to run,
It is warm and wonderful when new,
But when things turn you become blue,
That is when loving that one can really hurt,
Especially if you happened to be treated like dirt,
The life of love is never or will ever run smooth,
And becomes very boring when in a groove,
Love then wavers and weaves,
And soon is unsure then finally it leaves,
Love then leaves a shadow of doubt,
On a heart that is already having a bad bout,
This makes some just rather sad,
Some it is then said to have driven quite mad,
That is when words are said,
Which should have been put straight to bed,
Lovers may become friends,
Which is unfair on one in the end,
And to that one, Love will give
the reason of which rather not to live.

The Discarded
R.H.H.

In moonlight shadowed by ragged cloud,
Derelict I stand with rusting boiler, wheels and cab askew,
Seen as a scabied piece of scrap, incapable of thought,
A thing that can remember nought.
But I was built and driven by human hand,

None but my long gone footplate crew would understand,
That ghosts still linger in my cab,
And whilst they are there, the memories I still have.
Of racing along steel tracks that shimmered in the noonday
sun,
Beneath a windswept plume of smoke that marked my passing,
Through greens of spring and hues of autumn have I sped,
Beneath myriad stars in cold black night,
Passed silent houses without light,
Their occupants abed.
Sodden skies and whirling snows of winter have I faced,
Or grey, blinding fog, whose tendrils like some phantom's
creeping hand did wait,
To pluck my footplate crew away, and leave me to a sightless
fate.
Here I now abide, a rotting humbled hulk,
That stands until it in turn, becomes
Food for the bright blue torch to burn.
Knowing that when it reaches me,
My ghosts will flee.

Never Too Late
Dorothy Rawnsley

Just when you think that there isn't a soul
Who cares if you live or die,
When all your ambitions and final goal,
Become so much 'Pie In The Sky'.
Then, when the fire of your blazing youth
Has burned to an ashen pile,
Destiny waits 'til you're long of tooth,
Before making life worthwhile.

Cruel that all of your strength-filled years

Have turned, now, to days of rest,
But fortune decrees that you dry your tears -
And saves, for the last, the best.
So just when you think that the sands of time
Have finally run their span,
Remember - you'll ever be in your prime,
Whilst a woman still cares for man.

Summer On The Avon
Marion Cox

There on the grassy banks of Avon,
Where river sweeps to weir;
Where angler waits with wandlike rod
And dragonfly flits near,
A boat drifts lazily, lazily by
In the sunny heat of the afternoon,
And stops awhile at a tea-garden place
As the oarsman whistles a tune.
Drift along, drift along, over the Avon.
Lap along, lap along, feather your oars.
Pack up the tea-things, wind up the fishing line,
Sleep and dream of her, Avon is yours.

'Flu
Marjorie Dixon

I'm cooped up here in the house.
A Pause. I have to sneeze.
Ev'ry part of me just aches.
The pain in my poor knees!
My eyes just keep on running,

As also does my nose.
And now that it is bleeding
I must protect my clothes.

My head is quickly splitting
Itself right into two.
It's throbbing, throbbing, throbbing
No matter what I do.

And someone keeps on plunging
Sharp knives into my chest.
I'll go and get a hot drink
That seems to suit it best.

I'm cooped up here in the house,
I cannot do my walking.
And now I find I've lost my voice
Yes, me! Who enjoys talking!

Actor's Memories
Matthew Ould

'Mean Streets' said the taxi driver,
my final act came four minutes before.
'History now' cried the great dictator behind the door
Mummy drags my figure into his tomb
Inside Oscars turned to ash
at my age, Welles had dried up too.

Fangs connecting neck, green man chases John
ears aching toiling with the bells.
Antoinette on Scarlets back from the gallows.

'Juliet' - hand on heart - 'are you truly my girl?'
behind some mask I have played them all.

Autograph please - sorry - What's your role?
Sometimes I have gained acclaim and applause
Brookshaw and the one eyed creature the
placard said it All.

Tell Me In The Morning
David Blue

Are you sleeping?
Yes I was, but now I'm not
And now you've taken
The only warm spot
In the bed.

Were you dreaming?
Yes I was, well I think I was
But now I've lost it
And it's all because...
You've been drinking.

How was my night?
You did ask, I'm glad you did
And I'll tell you all
Of what was said
And then again.

Are you sleeping?
It's way past midnight
And you should get some rest

Because I think I might
Be falling asleep.

Jewel Box
Marguerite Walker

Everyone needs a box of dreams,
Then out they come, when life seems,
As though the sky has fallen down,
Obliterating the pathway,
Amidst great clouds of grey.
Then we should open that box of dreams,
Where we have kept our heart's desires.
Those dear, sweet dreams of earlier years,
Are our compass for the ways ahead.

Untitled
G B Mills

"Avast yer lubbers!" The cry is up.
Do yet think I'll go down to such a squall?
Cast yer eyes upon me Wrath, and think,
Would yers rather face me or the waters wall?
Then make fast those hatches and holes to port,
Or find yerself a task with hook and rope.
Ride the pitch and yaw me wayward lads,
Grasp hold the hawser and pull with 'ope.
Furl that fore sheet or feel my lash,
Steady that cask or you'll face the keel.
Up aloft, and give us our eyes, now move,
Out'a me way this is how to tame the wheel.

For this is me craft and vessel too,
I'll brook no slacking nor work askew.
I am the Captain of me ship fine lads,
So follow my lead and we'll pull through.

The Aching Arthritis
Kevin Fitzgerald

Anything I'd give to replace,
This curse upon the human race,
In all my joints you take your place,
Producing this dour face.

It is mornings I most dread,
The battle to rise up off my bed,
As I try to get up my bones go crack,
My joints cry out 'we're under attack'.
As I try to bend this poker back.

Then it's down the stairs my time I'm taking.
Thirteen steps they're all back breaking,
Creaking ankles, knees aquaking,
Oh what sounds my body's making,
It's enough to make the dead awaken.

Then it's into the kitchen it is my last stop,
Can I make it or will I drop?
I open the cupboard my chemist shop,
Medicine bottles, pills, it's got the lot,
Yes all these things to delight us,
In our battle with the aching arthritis.

In Innocence And Ignorance
Bryan J Roman

From my window ledge, a
Red sky of march I saw.
T'was as though, the sky
Had turned red with rage,
T'was as though, spinning
Ships of silver discs
Were burning the sky with
Heated rays.
Oh, what beauty, such the
Delight, an awesome sight
That set my heart alight.
A mere child who eyed the
Sky, as though the spectre
Was a November night, of
Fireworks exploding bright.
Unaware of the echoing
Voices of despair that were
Breaking around the globe.
A message that told of
The apocalypse of war.
This sea of red was not
Of twilights beauty,
But the sea of madness,
The stain of war.

An Extract?
Maureen Whiteley

He held my hand and looked at me,
a look I knew so well.

He may have smiled, or was it smirked
I couldn't really tell.
His hand came up and brushed my lips,
My breath it was a gasp.
My eyes they would not move from his,
My jaw was in his clasp.
Was it through some great desire
or fear that kept me still?
I only knew I could not move,
My stomach, it was ill.
He smiled once more and shook his head
My heart it missed a beat.
His face leant very near to mine,
Whilst tipping back my seat.
Oh no it can't be happeing
I've been through this before.
I've got to let him have his way
To fill my teeth once more!

Ode On The Death Of Princess Grace
Alan Ferster

Oh fairy princess of Monaco; Serene Princess Grace,
No span of years shall thy sweet looks efface;
She who held the Grimaldi Principality in sway
A tragic accident took her life away.

Once the world of Hollywood was her home;
To the south of France her steps did roam
There she wed her handsome prince
And lived in happiness ever since.

Silently the monks carry the body of Grace;
Death holds her to him in his cold embrace;
From a palace to the grave,
The final curtain - a farewell wave.

Remember readers of this verse where 'ere you are,
That wealth and honour bubbles are,
Long life a blast -
Only the good this princess wrought shall last!

A Pint Of Beer
N Montague

When things go wrong and will not come right,
Though you do the best you can,
When life looks black as the hour of night,
A pint of beer's yer man.

When money's tight and is hard to get
And your horse has also ran,
When all you have is a heap of debt -
A pint of beer's yer man.

When health is bad and your heart feels strange
And your face is pale and wan,
When doctors say that you need a change,
A pint of beer's yer man.

When food is scarce and your larder bare
And no rashers grease your pan
When hunger grows as your meals are rare
A pint of beer's yer man.

In time of trouble and endless strife
You have still got a darling plan
You still can turn to a brighter life -
A pint of beer's yer man.

The Long Way Home
Frances Jones

Folk say I was born a wanderlust
With travel in my soul,
For I've crossed the mighty continents
With a never-ending goal,
But as the years have slipped away
I feel weary now, my friend,
As I set sail for one last time
Toward my journey's end.

Yes, I've sailed uncharted waters
Where no man has been before,
Stood by giant waterfalls
And heard the thunderous roar,
Met the stateless and the starving
Seen sights to make one weep,
Crossed hostile, war-torn deserts
Where the watchful never sleep.

I've traversed the plains of Africa
And fallen 'neath their spell,
Dined with Kings and Princes,
Ah, such tales to tell,
But my heart yearns for another place
No more can I pretend,
As I sight the breezy shores of Albion,
I know I've found my journey's end.

Brainwashed
Vanessa Morton

T.V. kills our inspiration,
Making us a zombie nation,
Sitting in front of a box,
Like flocks of sheep,
Till, hypnotised we fall asleep.
The advert's envelope young children's minds,
Their jingles ousting nursery rhymes.
First word's may be a product they've seen,
Shouted at them from the corrupting screen.
Teenager's desensitised by violence, day after day,
Alter their games, and bring cruelty into play.
No-one converses on subjects that matter,
They just sit around getting fatter and fatter,
Absorbing the dross churned out every day,
In a totally indiscriminate way.
And maybe, one day, you will see,
A world full of mutes - all tuned to T.V.

My Sister's Bike
Lorraine Brown

Thanks for lending me your bike, it was very nice of you,
Oh, sorry that the brakes don't work, a nut fell off the shoe.
I felt so grand upon your bike, to ride it was a treat,
Of course that was before the springs - bounced out of the
seat.
I like the colour of your bike, a lovely shade of blue,
The scratch should cover easily, with a coat or two.
The crank arm came a little loose, I didn't want to meddle,
Now you've got a nice new block of wood for your left pedal.

I ting-a-linged upon your bike, it really did go well,
Oh, by the way, I have to say, shame about the bell.
You've really got strong mudguards and those stays are useful
things,
But with a small adjustment - they hold just as well with
strings.
Your bike just glides up all the hills, with those three speed
gears,
The gum that's where the bracket was, should hold them firm
for years.
I like the metal pump you've got, much better than the plastic,
The connectors got a little hole, I've filled it up with mastic.
I know you keep your chrome well greased, so to follow up
this caring,
I've made sure that I've done the same - I took it from a
bearing.
I've also cleaned the wheels for you, before they got too dirty,
A spoke came out the front one, but you've still got more than
thirty.
I've serviced your rear hub: look where the carrier fits,
You'll find some parts that were excess, they're in a bag
marked 'BITS'.
So you see I have looked after it, that black mark's only tar,
Now if I take up driving sis, can I lend your car?

Hill Climb
John Houston

Gravity of life pulls through limbs.
Umbilical incline pull on mind.
Hair blowing in cold wind,
warm earth's
wet
nose drips

cold sweat
catch
a
breath.
Wining wind winds, numbs
ear, eye rolls, over
misted view.
Life blood pumps,
from earth to sky.
Body feels good
floating
on solid ground.

Memories In My Attic
S Tideswell

Climb the ladder every day
Teddy and dollies all at play
My dear golly that's old George
Sits astride my old rocking horse
The carousel and music box
The kangaroo with Rupert the fox
Red coated soldiers all in line
Boots and buttons all a shine
Little monkey on a string
I had almost everything
Seeing them all makes me ecstatic
All fond memories in my attic

Coventry A Tribute
Violet Blumsom

Coventry, I saw you die
Beneath a blazing, burning sky.
Your medieval buildings fell
The cobbled streets were hades, hell.
No water left to quench the fires
That raged around your three great spires.
And yet among the smoke and stench
There was a spirit nought could quench.
And so you lived to rise again,
To salvage jewels that remain.
Trinity church, St. Mary's hall
Cathedral Tower that did not fall
But stands to guard the ruins yet
A prayer in stone we lest forget.

And Coventry held out her hands
to people from so many lands.
Now Mosques and Temples merge with spires.
Old faiths, new faiths fresh hope inspires
The citizens who are all part
of that strong beating valiant heart.

The Walk
Jim Leonard

The yellow sun hung in the cloudless sky
Somewhere a hound chased its prey
Our path ahead filled with colour
A thousand delicate flowers dancing in the breeze

178

You skimmed a stone on the shimmering lake
Watched it slide under the glassy surface
We breathed the clean air and smiled
Then marvelled at the greatness of our vision

We turned to go with our hearts at one
Hand in hand, satisfied within
We headed through the crumbling gate
And into the golden meadow

Its fragrance, so sweet and comforting
The warm breeze cooled us
Then we collapsed with satisfaction on the long, golden
grass
And butterflies guarded us from hidden invaders.

Lost Jennifer
Beardsmore

Songs for drinking, fist banging rhythms
Heavy drag foot dancing
Steely eyes, blank stares
Thick dusty mind curtains
Never to open, the play never to begin
Destinies lost in a fog
Sucking on a shifting mire
Flesh slithering through tunnels escaping
Through dim lit cracks seeking the dawn rebirth
Severed and strewn by the heat
White heat, white ice freezing co-existence
Imposters seeking hosts feast on the dried blood
Of lost souls shrieking in painful isolation

Indifferent, blind, filling the hollow cores with slime
Stunting roots, no new beginnings
Only the past, twisted, barbed, infected
Hooks deeps, tendrils crushing
Life's breath, gasping, rasping
Rattling

The Artist By The River
Susan F Handoll

The grey is uninviting
Cold and damp
I sit while waiting.

The morning's tide is high
Sheep are on the dyke.

Numb hands hold the brush
White paper holds colour
Fading as it dries.
Blue distant landscape merges
With the misty sky.

All is so still.

The curlew calls.
I watch the whirling flight
Of sandpipers momentarily disturbed.

The sun rises above the mist
An ever-changing scene
Another picture; clean white paper;
Peace.

Old People At Winter Time
Cheryl Laud

Old people at winter time
need lots of love and care,
most are weak and vulnerable
and need the love you can spare.

Make sure they have a hot meal
at least once a day,
keep them warm and care for them
and listen to what they say.

Old people are loving in their special ways
and love to talk about their golden days
So if you've got some love and time to spare
think of the old people who need your care.

Memories
Linda Bull

Now as our thoughts of the Gulf War subside,
Let's not forget our brave lads who have died,
Deep down in our hearts their memories won't fade
We'll never forget the brave soldiers they made
When sadness and sorrow, fill in our heart
The grief of our loved ones when they depart
They died as a hero, so gallant and bold.
Their sweet treasured memories, we always hold,
As tears fill our eyes, as we think of these lads.
Their memories are special, but they'll always be sad,
Those dear loving memories they left behind

For our dear loving sons, that were so loving and kind
We think of you now, as we did then
Although you were young you were very brave men
Our thoughts go out to their families and friends,
With our deepest sympathy that everyone sends.

Evening At The Cinema
Mary Spence

Three dimension silver screen
Acetate dream
Scrunch, scrunch of crisps and
paper bags
Tongues wag.
Excuse me, did I tread on your toe,
Didn't see it mate with the lights
so bloody low.
Fingers rummaging in bags of eats
Bums on seats
With loud crashing it starts
Drums with beats.
Unknown soldier killed in khaki
shadowed faces staring blankly
Youth's arm around girl just for
the night
Fleeting sight
Watching three dimensional screen
Acetate dream.

Dusk By The Forth
J Mitchell

Ancient stones, silhouetted blackly
Against the pale western sky.
The dark river, gun metal
Suffused with violet, and ghost grey,
A flock of yachts, like seabirds
Riding the waves.
Darkness, lights glide by, the
Massive bulk of tankers
Invisible, dark on dark.
Now is the time to listen, the
Rustling of leaves as creatures
Of the night set out to hunt. Squeeks,
The swish of wings passing low
And suddenly, the quiet is riven
By bloodcurdling screams
As daytime pussies
Proclaim their wild hatreds.

The Arab
Louise Allen

A detailed silhouette crests a dune,
Haloed by the setting sun.
See it's graceful dance as it gallops,
across the desert sand, that equine image.

Now with the sun at our backs,
We see the descendant of an ancient and fiery breed.
As he stops and raises up a foreleg in query,
We see his nostrils flare as he strains
the air current for our scent.

See his eyes that twinkle like the
stars in the clear desert sky.
Look, his forelock drifts across
his silken chestnut face.

He senses us and a spirited toss
of his arrogant head clears his sight.
Watch quietly as his muscles quiver
And he snorts his indecision.

See as he whirls about his delicate satin mane
And his streaming bannerlike tail.
His fine legs pumping to build up speed,
As he breaks into a gallop.

Do not be afraid as we lose him
In the descending darkness.
We can still hear his clean hard hooves
as he pounds the desert highways.

Judgement Day
Lee Patrick Conway

Desperate measures,
for desperate men,
The word is now mightier than the pen,
In nineties Britain
This is the case
Unemployment, vicious crime,
decline of the human race,
A downward spirit, too swift to halt,
Do you blame the politicians.

They say it's not their fault,
Is it the police, over population, the ozone layer,
is it the overpaid singer, football or tennis player
Try telling your children about perverts, Aids, nuclear
war,
You must be ever watchful,
they can't play on their own anymore,
There's no community spirit to see,
It's long gone, now fear is the key,
All we know for sure is that the world is in decline,
How much longer can we survive,
Will the sun continue to shine,
Not much longer,
A growing number say,
Mankind is heading for
Judgement day

Tender Eyes
Eileen Riches

Tender eyes shine from a face serene
Cherished lips to kiss in my dream
Arms held out to draw me near to a loving heart
filled with cheer

And to see those eyes shining only for me
To kiss those lips, tenderly
To be entwined in those loving arms is to surrender
completely to your charms

Reminiscing
Owen Curry

As I sit here reminiscing the summer of my boyhood
The good old happy days when we were free,
When school we used to run, in our barefeet having fun,
Fond memories you keep coming back to me.

In the evening we would wander round the Lough Erne's banks
so grand,
And see the fishing nets hung up to dry
We'd play marbles on the street, in baggy trousers and
barefeet,
But to old ways we must bid a fond goodbye.

At the weekend we would gather for the matinee in the Regal,
And gaze in wonder at the silver screen,
Sure we thought we're all cowboys like our heros on the trail
Now we know that was just another boyhood dream.
But sure youth it doesn't linger, like the wildbird on the wing,
It's gone and flown before you realise,
So when you're reminiscing of a time that you are missing,
Just remember boyhood was the greatest prize.

Despair
Helen Fraser

Death is an empty place
where time has no meaning
Death has a friendly face
that calls to me.
Calls to me like a lover yearning
for a fond embrace.
Death is a shroud

that covers me.
A black downy bed
that invites
eternal slumber.

The Bard's Prayer
Kevan Manwaring

I can count the stars backwards
catch moonbeams in my pockets
tiptoe betwixt blades of grass
hear the crack of dawn
gild my eyelids with silver linings
skate the rainbow with golden shoes
drink a fairy's tears gathered in my navel
converse with grasshoppers by clicking my toes
breathe in so hard that my hair is sucked back
pick up footprints by retracing steps
leap frog over low clouds
drink a stream
dry remember the name of every grain of sand
predict the path of shooting stars
make a ploughman's lunch with lunar cheese
sculpt the air with toothpicks
meet myself coming back before I get there
wish myself into tomorrow
& outrun my shadow
so
please believe me when I say
I am but a man of my word.

Speculation
David Richards

Throw a theory in the air
Watch it flutter, then beware
Lest the wind will blow away
All our thoughts of yesterday
That tremble in a thousand streams
Of silver bright, the stuff of dreams
Each new idea tries out its wings
Puffs out its breast and proudly sings
Of times that once were full of song
Where life rejoiced; could do no wrong
And tender the old leaf softly shook
As it drifted down the bubbling brook
Where time began its ceaseless play
Slowly flowing towards the day
When tarnish streaks beneath the gleam
And silence will take back the dream

Birthday
Lynn Harrison

Three days
into the sloth-like,
persistent white sleep
of a wintery new year
and out I came -
ejected and rejected,
covered in mucus and blood -
like a traffic accident victim;
penetrating, raping the atmosphere

188

with my screaming and fear,
as if I hated her for bringing me
into this weird, dying man-unkind world;
punching the air
with a tiny clenched fist
(always the anarchist) -
grasping at nothing with the other.
My subsequent reaction -
to rebel against my mother,
for nurturing the seed
that was now wet, sticky me -
for thrusting me
from warm, pulsating, secure womb
into the throbbing-headache world -
the tomb
of uncertainty.

Remember
T Wilson

The trees in the morning and barely a sound,
The misty cold, and polite chatter,
Stirrup cup, hats and gloves all the social graces,
Screaming, whirring of hunting dogs,
The smell of horses and freshly polished leather,
Immaculate red coats with gleaming gold buttons,
Bloody corpses torn apart with razor teeth,
Thundering hooves and sharp spurs
Seemingly impossible fences and terrified animals,
A long ride, and one small fox,
A shining intelligence showing through its exhaustion,
A small brown, living, breathing animal,

Who's lot is to be hunted down,
Horses and dogs who have no choice,
Fully grown, supposedly intelligent humans
Who have every choice,
A dirty, cold inhospitable day,
A dirty cold and uneven race,
The outcome not always foreseeable
And who has won,
Nearly always debatable.

Winter
B Bramma

Stark bare trees, and bitter weather,
Frozen pond, and iron-hard ground,
Tiny birds with fluffed up feather,
Cold grey silence, all around.
No more swallows flying high,
And scented flowers of every hue,
Gone the gentle butterfly,
And velvet rose-bud, tipped with dew.
Woodland creatures quietly sleep,
Beneath the snow, so soft and deep,
Waiting till the snowdrops ring,
Heralding another spring.
For nature gives a second chance
To flowers, and butterflies and trees,
Rest, their beauty to enhance,
If only, we could be like these.

Winter Flowering Cherry
E Janis Priestley

You've got it all wrong you silly tree.
This is winter.
Nine degrees of frost last night
And this morning, what do I see
Breaking open from tiny buds?
The palest of pale pink flowers
Tumbling down your leaf-bare branches
Clusters of tiny rose-hued showers.
Remember my surprise the first time
I gazed incredulously
At your inane absurdity?
That now gives me such delight.
Every year as November dies
First one bud opens, then a cluster
Until, little tree, you're dusted
With petals of fragrant blossom
A bride in an embroidered gown
Of silken pearls on Limerick lace.

The Suburban Fox
Sandra Booth

As I strolled along the paths one day
of this suburban place;
the body of a fox there lay
and there was peace upon his face.

I wonder what feelings moved his heart
before he met his fate;

if he'd ever been stung by jealousy's dart
or felt affection for his mate?

Whether he'd felt the kiss of Spring
or breathed in the scent of flowers;
or felt the joy that a birth can bring
or measured his life in hours?

Whilst he prowled around our street at dawn
I wonder if he yearned to be free;
or whether all these thoughts were born
with equanimity?

Think you, as I stare at his stiffening coat
with russet beauty blessed;
that all these feelings only float
within a human breast?

Dream Thoughts
V M Brackstone

Through my bedroom window,
Far beyond the dales,
Over the green belt, beyond the hills,
Faster than the crow bird sails,
Dreamy thoughts go out to you.

Dreaming thoughts of fantasy,
Together we'll fly to the stars,
Where the clustered Milky Way
Shines twinkling from afar.

In orbit, riding a rocket,
Our minds will be as one;
Skimming over the moon, and back again,
To home once more we'll come.

The dawn is breaking through Love.
Resting our dreams in sleep,
To climb the highest star above
In future nights to keep.

The Lover
Neiloy Ghosh

Anxious, he awaits his lover's return;
Ignoring distraction by bland broadcast
Where bronze teen idols act idyllic lives.
Own limp virility consigned to the past:
Emasculated by matrimonial knives
Forged in a furnace of searing burn.

Excursion, coition - they seem so rare.
Twenty creeping ages elapsed, since
Love became duty, respectability.
And Sunday nights with the Larkins,
Became enthralling opportunity.
Doesn't he desire, dream or dare.

To stare upon fear's fathomless pools
And skim stones across the forbidden body.
To escape and assume lost aspiration
Bequeathed to love's prizes: Wet with folly
And defiance, yet distant reflections;
Rippling and spurning the cautious rules.

That strangled the gasps of originality
And stifled romance's claim for life.
Yet love survives; coughing and spluttering,
Behind a blaring box with man and wife,
Sitting, offering silent muttering.
Love constant amidst spirit's fatality.

Candle Light
Allyson Ward

The room seems dark and silent
In the stillness of the night
But burning in the background
Is a flickering candle light

The flame it looks so gentle
A magic of it's own
An image of perfection
Yet a feeling of unknown

It stands with so much gracefulness
Power, warmth and might
It glows, a glow like sunset
This beauty, brings us sight

It is therefore a conflict
To the human mind
Why this wonderous specimen
Must burn out of it's life

Life
Edna Hay-Helps

The minutes pass like hours today,
As doubts and fears cloud my way,
Today, tomorrow seems to be
An even greater uncertainty.

And yet the roses bloom the same,
Their petals falling in stormy rain,
Sweet perfume lingering in the sultry air,
And tomorrows rosebuds already there.

The summer breeze blows through the trees,
Murmuring and whispering to the leaves,
If I can listen with inner peace,
I will hear the voice of nature speak.

But if I listen when Soul does speak,
I will hear the solace that I seek,
For in it's silent wordless call,
It that sacred Being within us all.

Untitled
Martin Schoenbeck

How can a man admit to being lonely -
His mind confused; his body company
How can a man admit to being afraid -
His aggression deceives, only his eyes falter.

How can a man be so close, but yet so far -
He talks of love, life and death; he cannot truly share.
How can a man be so timid but yet so arrogant
He hides in a facade of self-denial

How can a man so full of rich experience be so devoid of
passion
His emotions always sacrificed by fear
How can a man be afraid of the end
When he hasn't the courage to allow a beginning?

How can a man choose to die alone
Is this really courageous or borne of fear?
How can a man's heart be so lonely
His mind confused; his body has company.

An Enigmatic Female
Steven McElroy

You tease and you taunt,
You flirt and you flaunt,
You're attractive, sexy and so nice.

You're open and friendly,
Warm and inviting,
You allure, please and entice.

You're alive and exciting,
But in many ways frightening,
Yet seem controlled and aware.

You have a free spirit,
Carefree and emotionally with it.
Which I can only admire and stare.

Your presence it haunts,
Your body it taunts,
But you're not flash or debonair.

Your feelings are deceiving,
I very rarely see them,
They're handled with charisma and flair,

You're captivating and riveting,
You seem to have just everything,
But are you so divine?

You come close, yet keep your distance,
But you can easily break male resistance,
A beautiful enigmatic female whose not mine.

Moray Firth Dolphins
Jill Bennett

The fish shoal
and tip to tail
the dolphins follow.
Shadowed acrobats,
sleek, supple,
playful.

Aquatic jesters,
they wear a

timeless smile
and entertain the
watchers from
the shore

who, drawn to
the edge
of a growing
Highland land
listen to the
siren's sound

free, enticing
and in tune
with nature,
captivating the
heart, with
a soulful longing.

The Voice
Darren Spruce

The voice of deceit
The voice of lies
The voice of trust
& the one which cries

Listen;
Command the words of knowledge
& end their learning,
Whisper the words of emotion
& hide their wanting.

Affectionate words need tender thoughts.

Caress the tongue of love
& embrace its desire,
Scold the tongue of wrath
& reap its anger.

Hypnosis of our ears; no fears.

With sensual delicate talk, I've fallen,
venerable moulding lips entrance.
As I listen to your mild medication,
your voice continues to dance.
(You are my last chance).

This Liquid
Bernard Samuel

This Liquid
unlocks
a catalogue of wealth
a vocabulary of latitude

bereft of
punctuation
parameters
and hindrance

words searching
in every orifice
without discipline
without brakes

crumpled
unfinished
unread
unpublished

This Liquid
unlocks
a catalogue of wealth
a vocabulary of latitude.

A Late Autumn
Connie Esterson

Nature fooled by the balmy air,
The green so loathe to go,
Barely a wrinkled leaf to fall,
Seduced by the kiss of sun.

Creeper spreads its fiery red
Along a mellowed wall,
Its glory gone in a flash of days,
A mirage in the green.

Beneath a veil of liquid gold
The trees hide winter faces;
Overnight, it seems, the fallen leaves
Lie crisping on the path.

Colour lingers still - the rose that blooms
Defiant to the last, stubborn leaves
That cling to naked bark -
But the wind comes chill
In the teeth of the dying year.

I Loved You
David Beisty

Do you live?
Do you lie?
Do you laugh?
Do you cry?

Do you want?
Do you need?
Do you hurt?
Do you bleed?

Do you hope?
Do you care?
Do you mind?
Do you dare?

Do you speak?
Do you tell?
Do you love?
Do you hell!

Your Life Should Be For You
Donna Masterson

Learn well your boundaries
In the game of life that you play
You have the choice to explore
Or at home you can stay.

You are allowed to take chances
to be different or loud
You have the choice to be placid
Or to stand out in a crowd.

You can choose your own happiness.
Or behind another's life you can hide
You can choose the friends that you keep
Or the secrets you confide.

So if you listen to your needs
Instead of living through another
There will be no unconquered boundaries
As peace of mind - You will discover!

The Lighthouse
Frances M Field

It was a velvet night, soft and warm
But the waves lapping the shore
Drew me from my thoughts.
I was alone save for that beam
Which rapidly swept the sea
Beckoning, swinging its arm
As if to envelope and draw me.
The tide, understanding,
Brought the sea nearer
Until it caressed my feet.
The water held my body
And gently rocked me in its swell.
Above, the stars nodded
In the heavy, waiting sky.

Then the whirlpool caught me
Twisted and turned me
Chilled and burned me
Until the blood pounded in my ears
And my lungs shrieked soundlessly.
Down I went, so deep I felt
I would never return.
Then up and up from a great depth,
Gasping as the red light splintered on the sea
Which calmed and held me.

A Friend For Life
Elsie Monks

You are fortunate to have a friend
To share your problems and fears,
A good friend who will follow you -
All the way, down the years.

Not only will he share your happiness
But your griefs and sorrows too,
Whatever happens to you tomorrow
Your friend will be there to comfort you.

Surely this si the kind of friend you need
One who is faithful, true and kind,
A friend whom you can rely on -
Who will give you peace of mind.

Supposing your faith begins to wain
Your friend causes you to frown,
An even greater Friend awaits you
He will never let you down.

So be careful how you choose your friend
Whether you be young, or old,
A good Friend is a Friend for life
He will bring you joys untold.

Little Scab
Calvin Clarke

O little scab upon my knee
How I wonder much of thee
Like some band-aid, you're about
Stopping blood from leaking out.

Me thinks that thou art all congealed
Until my graze has fully healed
I cannot wait that long to find
You've left me with a scar behind.

So as not to hurt my knee
I'll pluck thee off as quick can be
Then pop you in my mouth and chew
And so I shall recycle you.

Our Tree
Moira Brown

Our tree stood tall
We passed it every day
Upon the bark -a-
Heart was carved

Your name and mine entwined
I loved that tree
I really did
I touched it every day

I felt it was a good omen
Our love - for all to see
We got married - emigrated
Fell out of love - divorced

Back home to my parent's
To get myself in order
Three months go by
I smile again

I feel a little stronger
I'll take a walk - look for our tree
Maybe - even touch it
But! like our love - our tree has gone

Cut off in our prime
A bitter sweet memory
I wonder -
Is it a good omen - can I love again.

Painting A Summer's Morning
Roy V Vaughan

Ghostly grass, phantom fields,
a pale grey wash over English wealds.
Dissected trees that weep false tears
skillfully applied by mist; now fears

that the lemon watercolour sun
that overslept, will have to run
undignified, to take his place
and start the day with perspiring face,
so splashing with the palette's paint
each solitary leaf, without restraint.
Never was a monarch so bejewelled,
(that we could only watch enthralled)
the change to multicoloured hues
that filled the senses 'til they, imbued
could not properly greet the wondrous dawning
of an Essex, summer's morning.

The View From My Window
Barbara Pearce

Let us never feel the need to cry,
Or mourn those that were taken from us,
By murdering men who knew no right.
For the sake of the world we beg.

Let us see that guns have no place in life,
That torture can be part of our past,
And that people can live with each other.
For the sake of the world we beg.

Let us be able to walk in green fields,
And know that our children are safe,
Free from AIDS, UV rays and pollution.
For the sake of the world we beg.

Let us stop for a minute and think
About the pain that grows in our heart,
And reflect on the view from our window,
Before the curtains close, we beg.

Wife At A Party (Tit For Tat)
Lynn Senior

He lights her cigarette I watch the flame
as it flickers up then dies again.
He laughs, too loudly, then whispers something I don't
hear
This goes on
at the party all night long
His back to me
Still, he knows that I can see
Oh but you are happy now my love
for we shall drive home in silence
But later on make love with tenderness not violence
For I may have hurt you earlier talking
of all the things you lack
But it's ok now
You have paid me back.
Tit for Tat my love
It's always Tit for Tat...

On Looking The Wrong Way
Graham Bloss

So many avenues I've searched,
Through music and my books,

And all my heroes are now gone,
So should I cease to look?

Long were the black and rain-lashed roads,
So dark the full-leaved wood,
No paths would lead where I would go,
And few I felt were good.

I knew that none would step with me,
Along those stony ways,
Nor stride along the high sea-cliffs,
Around the stormy bays.

I turned to look back at the sun,
Just as the summer changed,
And in my head a thought was born,
So obvious, yet strange.

Through all the verse and rhymes I wrote,
I never seemed to see,
That I am just the sort of man,
I always wished to be.

Job Vacancy
Irvin Gomersall

Think of a DIRTY... Thankless task,
Then take one... Ten times worse,
With HALF your pay... More Discipline,
And family life, accursed.

Then take a shattered, Human wreck,
Shaped something like a man,
And with gentleness and loving care...
Restore him, if you can!

Still, do not rest... But go and learn,
And then go learn some more.
For every lesson's vital...
There's not one you Dare ignore.

Then, just like Punchinello,
Learn to smile, when you could cry,
And attend the other fellow,
And gently wipe HIS eye.

If you think you have the Character,
To do this... and much worse
Then maybe... Just Maybe, you've the makings
That are needed... For a NURSE.

Walter's Desire
Christine Moyse

Walter was a woodlouse,
Who had just one desire.
To see how much he could eat,
Whilst sprawled out in front of the fire.

His mother got wise to this,
And said "You'll get too fat,
Now run round the garden a hundred times",
But Walter didn't like the sound of that!

Now smarties he ate hundreds
And boiled sweets he ate lots,
And very soon had toothache,
As well as covered in spots.

But the ultimate insult came,
When he put on his Sunday Best,
for it no longer fitted him,
Not even his new string vest.

Walter realised he had to slim
And that he'd been a bit greedy.
So all the sweets that he had left,
He shared out amongst the needy.

Then he started jogging round the block,
And gave up cakes and beer.
And rumour has it round his town,
That he's won "Slimmer of the Year!"

Red Rose
A M Bower

Man must surely be very pleased
To take from God with such arrant ease
From among the gifts which he bestows
The beauty and splendour of a Red Rose.

To capture as long as the season
The wonder for and the reason
Ever protected from wanton hand
With thorny bush to withstand.

The softness of it's petals show
Velvet texture we love to grow
Surely the most beautiful flower
One could find in any bower.

An artist will try to capture - for he knows
The rich velvet beauty of a Red Rose
Not forgetting it's fragrance too
Unlike any other when kissed by dew.

So let us for small mercies be grateful
Give thanks to God when we feel tearful,
Just take the pleasure with the one who grows
The splendid beauty of a Red Rose.

Suffer The Little Children
Ellen Walker

Too many words have been spoken,
Too many tears have been shed
Still the killing and maiming continues
While the heart of a country is bled.

Too many children are dying,
Too many families left crying.
Still the wars and the bombings continue
And the heart of a country is bled.

Our children are the heart of a nation,
The flowers - the fulfillment of love,
Yet they are the ones first to suffer
From a hatred nourished on blood.

Too many words left unspoken,
Too many tears still to shed,
When the flowers of love lie broken
And the heart of a nation is dead.

Spider
Marilyn Haynes

I am not really goodlooking
I think I lack the charm,
Just to be a spider
To lure you into my arms.

I often try some tactics,
To make you want me more,
Just to be a spider
To lure you through my door.

If I was a tricky spider
I would do some terrible deeds
You never would forgive me
I know this
For I sure know your needs.

So come my man into my web,
Be happy and content with me,
We could be so happy,
I am sure so try me and see.

We could spin our web together,
All golden sparkle and bright
We could spin it all by day
To lie comfortable at night.

Jealous Much
Melissa Terras

The situation now; old emotions
Are tangled, twisted, though they once strained plain,
As knots replace embroidered devotion
Should I see you hold another. I shan't feign
Love, for never felt it, and dishonest
Comments often lead to further lies.
I resurrect no utterance or promise
Nor send dead fondness (rotted) in disguise.
To say I do not feel: I am counterfeit,
As jealous ties prove that your love I miss,
But countless others also could have sent it
And can provide companionship, a kiss.
It is not you but close friendship I lack.
Though missing it, I'd never have you back.

I Promise
Sadie McKendrick

To share -To care - To understand
To love - To listen - To lend a hand
To forgive - To forget - & To endure
To help - To advise - To reassure
To have faith - To give hope - To be charitable
To give shelter - To give food - To any individual
To be honest - To believe - To be fair
To have courage - To keep going - To always be there
If anyone should call on you
Welcome them, be they black/white or Hindu
If people would ignore the colour of ones skin
This world would be - A much better place - To live in.

Holidays
Eveline Cook

Weather worrying holidays
Six weeks in a row
Shall we try the coast today
or walk along the moor?
Hunks of tasty sandwiches
buttered in a rush
Chase into the garden
grab salad by the score, then
apples, cheese and sausages
more - and more - and more -

Kettle stove and teapot
Games and books to store
Just in case the rain pours down
or a breakdown is in store.
Rugs and balls, buckets and spades
Swimsuits and towels galore
Extra socks and footwear
more - and more - and more

Packed into the car the
list seems never ending
I wonder what I shall forget
or should I take the mending?
The days stretch out before us
I swoon into my seat
I hope we go a long, long way
so I can sle-ee-eep!!!!

Mummy's Little Helper
Derek J Haggan

No fidget fingers fumbling, finding funny things to do
No little brush and dustpan, and worse, no little Sue.

'Can I help you mummy?' she recalled as her eyes glazed
She wiped away a teardrop hardly seeing through the haze

Pushing pulling, picking up
Remembering how Sue broke that cup

Laughing playing
Never straying...

Not here now...

Mummy's little helper
It seems she's gone away
Another doll, another ball
Another smudge on bedroom wall
One more tear,
Another fear
And then she felt a fool...
It was her only daughter's
First full day at school.

Changes
The Past... For Deborah
Neil Fulford

You Shit,
My life became a haze,
spent in a complex maze,

my hopes all burnt then razed,
You Shit,
I tried not to give a toss,
about the life I'd lost,
I put up with your frost.
You Shit,
I became emasculated,
I thought it fated,
and left if undebated.
You Shit,
From my life I wanted more
than your dominance, hoar,
you made me the bore.
You Shit.

And now, finally free,
with greater knowledge of me,
I thank you gratefully.

But still, think you, a shit.

God Made It All
Eric Wyld

God made the wooded slopes
He made the rolling downs
He made the hills and valleys
And he gave all nature gowns.

By His word He brought forth
Trees the fruit the flowers
Sunshine and the daylight
The sweet and steady showers.

Pasture land where cattle graze
Or roam the hills and dales
Streams of running water
Down swiftly through the vales.

By word they were created
From His heavenly throne
Created man was given
This lovely earth for home.

A Winter's Night
Marilyn V Brown

I will never forget, on that cold winter's night
When I saw the beautiful orb of the moon,
Rising from the horizon, shining so brightly,
Casting its light on the sparse snows below.

The night was still, until, a car sped by, disturbing the silence;
A man walking his dog, turned to stare at the noise
Breaking his peace.
The car vanished from sight, into the night.

The silence closed round,
An owl hooted distantly, a coyote yipped, re-echoing around.
The man and his dog walked on, their breath
Freezing into droplets in the cold night air.

Majestically, the moon rose higher into the sky
Extending its light further over the great Vast Land
Covering prairies, the rolling hills and mountains so free,
Brightening scattered houses and ranches

Nestling at the base of the rolling hills,
Their lights twinkling
In depths of night.
Temperatures dropped, frost descended

So crisp and cruel,
To damage the plants
Left out by an unwary homesteader,
Becoming blackened and shrivelled by morning.

Today
Stephen R Harrup

This may not be the time for recriminations
And I will not ask for hasty explanations
We should part in a civilised way
There is too much pain to be hurt more today.

Sorry has been said too many times before
"I'll do better" and excuses by the score
But things have never improved have they
And things cannot get worse than they are today.

Your eyes cannot hide the hard decision you made
This break up is overdue and must not be delayed
Your smile is forced, the mood is grey
And parting is the lesson learnt today.

This does not seem real, but it is so true
This is the moment when it is not us, but me and you
Will we ever forgive what we did not say
Will I ever see you again after today.

No, recriminations are not what we should share
Only silence should hang in this heavy air
And there is no point my begging you to stay
For the end has arrived, and you leave today.

The Immigrants Song
Margaret McIntosh

Many young lovers forced to leave their home,
will dearly remember the place they call their own,
and how the Moon to impress them would brighten the Sky,
to compliment the glint in a young girls eye.
But the magic that shone came not from on high,
but came from the light that twinkled in her eye.
And although their parting was sealed with a kiss,
they knew they'd return on a night such as this,
when the magic of the evening shall beckon and call,
then lovers will return again, beneath the Moon of Donegal.

And no land will be fairer, nor place held more dear,
for the shores that they love will always be here.
For the Moon is a stranger that shines far away,
on a land of toil, at the end of each day,
and the streets that are walked mark out the miles,
of heartache and longing, for those homely smiles.
Till the magic of evening shall beckon and call,
then lovers will return again, beneath the Moon of Donegal.

And no matter how far, and no matter how long,
home will always be remembered in song,
from the mountains to the shores their memories will drift,
with the pull of the land that first gave them birth,
till the magic of the evening shall beckon and call,
then lovers will return again, beneath the Moon of Donegal.

One Moment In Time
Sylvia I Moore

If I could take one moment in time
It would be this:
To look into my lover's eyes.

If I could take one moment in time
It would be this:
To feel the sweetness of his kiss.

If I could take one moment in time
It would be this:
To feel his gentle caress.

If I could take one moment in time
It would be this:
To feel the comfort of his love.

If I could take one moment in time
It would be this:
To remain forever where two become one.

Little Bird
Angela Newlands

A creature small and very swift
That floats above on high
I wish, I was that little bird
Just to sail up in the sky

It seems so lonely and care-free
Just stopping here and there
When people try to capture it
It doesn't seem to care

On a window ledge, it does often perch
Just to say hello!
It does not stop for long I guess
For it is always on the go

It spreads its long and feathered wings
Just before it goes
I wonder where it came from
But no one ever knows

A Time To Gain
Lorraine Hislop

Jewelled tiara of close knit length,
Jagged edges of cultured rhymes
Just a kiss of expert lips,
A step in time.

Forlorn images of time gone by,
Farthest thresholds of childhood dreams,
Carpets, angered, bloody, bare,
A sign, a time to scream.

Angels watching, head to toe,
Anarchy and a raging skull,
Lost horizons slipped and past,
A facade so dull.

Lord be with me step to step,
Lrd have mercy, hear me weep,
Lord give sorrow, softened edge,
A time to sleep.

Tainted mercury billious gut,
Tangled web of fear and pain,
Lord listen, hear the voice within,
A time to gain.

God's Gifts
Patricia Moore

How refreshing the rain
'Though it's sometimes a pain!
How warm the sun
That lets us have fun!
How lovely the moon light
That lights up the night
How brilliant the sun rays
That light up the days
How lovely the stars
That watch in night hours
How sparkling the sea
That's lovely to see
How blue is the sky
Above us so high
How curly the river
That winds it's way thither
How regal the swan
As it glides down the river
How pretty the rainbow

With colours so bright
How pretty the butterflies
Who on their wings fly
Take stock of these things
Before God gives you wings!

Hollywood Sweetheart
James Rogers

Though many men before and after,
Have made their peers resort to laughter;
Men through time have made us tearful,
Whilst countless hundreds require us fearful.
But the subtle need to laugh and cry,
For now and ever is you and I.

I don't know how and never will,
To let you know I love you still.
If through the mist upon the street
Appears my Catherine ever sweet,
The gloom around me swept aside
I find my feelings hard to hide.

The days though long are filled with thoughts,
Yet come the night entranced in dreams,
I lie awake and think it through,
And lonely though my future seems;
I ponder nothing else but you.

Demise Of A Miser
Kathy Fisher

He died alone and weary,
he'd never wed, the poor old miser.
Kept his money to himself.
Died rich but none the wiser.

Rich but poor and dying,
he'd never loved or tasted life.
He had the means and plenty,
but not to share it with a wife.

None came to pay him last respects.
There weren't even any flowers.
He'd never shown emotion but,
a tear fell in his last hours.

He thought he'd take it with him,
the surprise came when he died.
The scavenging vultures took it,
when the hearse took him for a ride

He'd never given of himself,
sharing was unknown.
Never talked to anyone.
He died lonely and alone.

The Snow
L Wall

The snowfall whitewashed everything
It made things clean and pure

The world had been reborn again
But nothing is too sure.

The rain came down, the snow turned black
The icy roads were fatal
The skid, the crash, the screams, the blood
The tangled, twisted metal.

Three people died.
The snow fell.

The snowfall whitewashed everything
It made things clean and pure
The world had been reborn again
But nothing is too sure.

First Anniversary
Denis Tuohy

There will be many battles, so you said,
Smiling as though you feared no battle ground.
That afternoon, in the breeze fondling the curtain
Fireflies of sunlight danced their way
From my caressing arm to your stroked skin.

Your prophecy has proved itself. The wounds
Are chronicled in tears and elegies
Whispered in the baffled aftermath.
But the space we vie for is common ground.
Our stars command it. Flowers will grow here.

Creature Of The Night
Penny Mather

A silhouette against the night sky
He calls to his mate
It is late
(I will bring food before long, before morning)
Sleep safely in your den
Away from man
Listen to my warning
Do not venture above ground
Though the carpet of bluebell
Yet unopened
Provide your cover
Make no sound
Creature of the night
E'er long you will provide
For your family
Move swiftly through the bracken
Go quickly to the old oak tree
She waits for thee
Beneath the spreading roots
Safely.

Camera Obscura
Helen Luson

All night this room of incarceration
Squats warm and waiting,
Flame-furious dragon breathing
A seethe of papers.
At daybreak it deprives me of me.

One snide window like a boss-eyed Cyclops
Yawns at the wide world,
Ignores the secret angst of spring,
Stormcoat of winter,
The melody in a dreamer's soul.

This room has never entertained angels,
Never knowingly
Stepped beside the words that tango
In a wilder way,
Never let its guilt show, so to speak.

Secretarial segacity drips
From the disguised sky,
Computers sigh like a heat wave,
Lash the unwary,
Reward the weary with a rainbow.

But when will the trade ever stop
In half-baked rainbows?

Dawn
Gemma Parkes

The fluty, melodious tune of the blackbird
Opens the rich chorus of birdsong.
The early mist lifts from the valley
Giving way to clear, sweet air,
As shiny yellow sunlight spills over the horizon
To paint the world with soft, warm colour.
The clear, tranquil river reflects the blue sky
Which is scattered with white cotton wool clouds.

227

Finches and skylarks chase through the meadow
While the drowsy sheep graze on the hillside;
The grass they are eating
Twinkles with droplets of morning dew.
And as I walk through crocuses and snowdrops,
I realise that in minutes
The countryside has bloomed from sleepy stillness
Into an ocean of timeless treasures:
A festival of life.

Humpty Dumpty
(In the style of John Betjeman)
Vicki Vrint

The morning passed by much too slowly
For Humpty (who sat on the wall).
He was lonely - he felt isolated.
No letter, no telephone call.

He looked at the town from his viewpoint
Saw the factories, their fumes - heard the bell.
First he turned to the east and saw houses
Then he turned to the west - and just fell!

Passers-by came and cried "Fetch the medics!"
With the call-out at five pounds a head?
They soon realised it would be expensive
So they called men and horses instead.

'Though they all tried their hardest to save him
He too easily gave up the fight.
A death caused by fate? or by boredom?
(A sadly suburban blight)

Nothing... But The Rain
Jacqueline Kent

Lost and lonely,
Ghostly pale
She stood beneath a star
And watched the rain
As it fell
And shattered on the street like glass,
Like her fragile life
Her precious dreams -
Crumpled, torn and left for dead...
Words echoed in her mind
"It's not your fault"
As she smiled at nothing
But the pouring rain
As it mingled
And danced with the same salty tears
Falling like blood
From a dead girl's face.

Life
E Blanton

About grief I learned the hard way
Of the damage that it does,
To your constitution when
You lose the one you love.

You think that fate's against you
That tomorrow you'll still be hurt,
Your eyes red rimmed with crying
Your body pained and taut.

You drag yourself about life's chores
Not wanting to live yourself,
You feel life has trampled on you
Leaving you battered on the shelf.

Then quietly, as time goes by
You scarcely feel the change,
You smile again, you see the sun
You don't feel so deranged.

The suddenly, life seems good again
You can share things and enjoy,
The glories this world has to offer
To every girl and boy.

To The Disdaining She
Stephen Blake

Not mere abstinence
This lack of response;
No lively bulldozer has
Shoved a handsome catastrophe
Face first into your's
That you could not scrape
Together thought to send me one
Word, even an offhand no.

Anyway, no ink
Could redeem you, no
Intermediary defend;
Your silence is too pertinent.

And I am no pug
Ugly toy, my sweet,
My dear, my pet, nor a slavish
Rodent mooning after the
Big cheese (which you are
Not) that I cannot
Discard your name, casually
Lift my tail and eye you up

For the last, and trot
Far superior
From your basket; the lair of
The haughty She, the Cat's Mother.

Gentle Giants
Daniel Luke Moskal

In very deep sleep,
My spirit or mentality cannot ignore physical space,
Or physical discomfort
To sense danger, to picture mentally,
A warning of danger, both ancient and modern
These aliens poison my friendship and love
For my tongue has a bitterness of mind, they have no heart
Beware of their false judgements, look to their associates,
Who reap the rewards.
In the interior of continents
Ivory lays scorched by an African sun,
Where jungle eaters strip off everything
That grows and makes black-money
No sanctuary for 'Gentle Giants';
To picture a calf mourning
For her lost blood-stained security,
Lying silently in an African bush,

Burnt by a Gemini sunset.
An extra arm gently caresses with love and tender
To speak: "AWAKE MOTHER, AWAKE!":
She desperately murmurs in a silent, un-moving ear.
Inborn action of an endangered species,
Whose life was wasted for the sake of greed.

The Wounds Of Time
Gavin Paul Carter

A memory caught upon the tapestry of time,
dark grey and faded, silent eyes, forgotten stare
A smile so warm from lips that tender kissed upon my face
but now so still beneath a silver frame that only I can share.
Forever encased in a beauty so sublime,
dulled in black and white,
a picture framed from flash of light,
that lay so still, beneath the film of a ghostly silver mist,
where no creases in her tender flesh did show the wounds of
time.
An ageless vision, grim shadows cannot cover,
although you sleep and forever keep inside God's realm of
eternal bliss.
I remember sunlit years when you and I were lovers,
so upon the polished crystal glass I imprint a loving kiss.

The Story-Teller
Alex Pascall

I'm the story-teller who likes to rhyme,
Telling all types of stories from time to time.
Some are folk tales from Grandma and Dad,
Some are funny ditties from me Auntie Maud.

I'm the story-teller. I tell them through song
With the beat of the drum, moving up and down.
I'm the story teller with imagination,
Full of style in my recitation.
I'm the story-teller who tells no lies -
Just a little disguise as I dramatise.

So I'll close with a ditty from me old Aunt ie:
Set no molasses, catch no flies!
Crick, crack, the wire bend,
And the story end.

Mirror Mirror
Michelle Adamson

"Mirror after mirror
I see a girl in repose,
Blonde hair framing blue eyes
Gentle pink cheeks, red mouth,
No smile, no expression
Yet beautiful and knowing.

And then I see it's me
Or how I'd like to be,
Constantly looking at the girl
To make sure she's still alive;
In there somewhere.

Reassurance of something tangible
But not definable
Touchable, but always on the other side.

We walk towards each other and we touch
I can feel her loneliness and sadness
But can reach no further
Than the cold surface contact."

Love Poem
F R Wagstaffe

She came into my life a year ago.
I liked her stripey T-shirts and the way
She would amble in late and self-consciously
Bang her bag quite hard against her hip.
Later I saw her out at a club,
In black jeans wearing the shadows,
And it seems, felt out of place,
But the darkness, I thought, suited her.
I tried to smile, she looked uncomfortable.
That night I fell out with the world,
(Which happened often)
And then I went to war.

Strange to think our courtship happened
Mostly in my head; I wouldn't speak and you would turn
away.
We managed a greeting in the corridor,
I knew you wondered what I was smiling for;
I knew and thought I was being coy.
There were brief moments of joy,
But over all, looking back, I just felt good;

- I still do.

Frost Paths Through The Clearing
John Craig

You close your eyes to the night
that is frozen between winter and space
like an unknown hunger
but the stars still pierce your eyelids
and your dreams are permeated
by the intensity of their bitterness.
When you start from your sleep,
you can feel the night sky deep inside you,
each constellation hurting at its own existence,
their distances invading every part of you;
it taints you with its stillness
and you carry it into the colourless day,
shuddering with the thinness of your life
as the stars tear beneath your skin.

Rejection
Mary Farrant

You have been rejected,
can you still survive
unwanted one.

There is no work for you,
what will you do?
unwanted one.

Huge panes of glass
let you clearly see
the things you cannot have.

They tempt you so
don't smash the glass
you will be condemned.

You have been rejected,
can you still survive
unwanted one.

You can survive unwanted one,
Life has a purpose for you,
don't ask me what it is
just survive.

Benediction
Pearl M Goodall

I remembered you, In my
prayers last night,
Not on my knees, With my
eyes closed tight,
But, Standing at my
window,
Gazing at the evening
star,
I asked God to bless
you,
Where-ever you are.

Love's Faithful Ones
Kevin P Cryan

We view with just a little envy
Those to whom love seems easy,
Those who, like ourselves, meet quite by chance
But settle for what chance has offered
- Some near approximation of love's devotion.

Not for them the drawn-out rituals
Or hours devoted to a minute ecstasy;
Not for them the trials
That moves love nearer to perfection.

For both of us
There can be nothing more
Than this vague longing,
This suppressed desire for new beginnings
When love is simple impulse
And points in no direction.

We may sit, and look,
And listen to each other,
Smile across this table
On which wine glasses weep;
But far away - in other places -
There's love's unfinished business
That will not let us be.

Amazon
Deborah McQuaid

Watch her stand, naked.
Unhappiness streams from her nose,
Her hands shredded and red
Eyes glow and petrify,
the hate has buried the bloom.
Now I see burns and stone.
That mouth castrates taste,
Lips peel and bleed.

The bones lubricate the blood,
Tears nourish and swallow, swallow.

Under her hair she is queen.
This skull is tight and hard
Swimming strongly under curls.
Shining, thick black hair, glows
above the pain, topping the mess.

Dogs
K Bonser

A dog is such a special thing,
They're endless to the joy's they bring.
All they ask is a meal a day
In return give affection and play.
They lie by the fire or the seat of your lap,
Join you in bed for an afternoon nap.
They give protection right through the night,
Any intruders they'll put up a fight.

They beg for their food, and sit when they're told,
They're tender and loving, they're brave and they're bold.
Their tails start wagging at the sight of a lead,
They're loving and loyal,
They're one hell of a breed.

Have You Ever Really Used Your Eyes?
Kirsty McGreevy

Have you seen a pond?
have you seen the fish?
have you ever caught one
To put upon your dish?

Have you seen the animals
Scatter around the bush?
Have you seen the squirrel
say to her young
"Hush hush?"

Have you seen the birds
Building a nest?
Have you seen the mice
From their work
Have a rest?

Have you ever really used your eyes?

Worries
Elizabeth Bisset

Personally in my family we were dealt a heavy blow.
I tried looking happy my inner-feelings too ashamed to show.
When sobbing to myself my family, why now!
I got to thinking I'm feeling sorry for myself and how!
I then started thinking of all the hospitals in the land
Where Doctors and nurses daily just have to let that patient
go...
I thought of all the bad news, police and emergency services
have to give.
I then decided that my life was not that bad at least I was
lucky
I had laughter and joy to give and many reasons to want to
live.
My heart still feels heavily laden but at least I know that if I
want to go for a walk unaided I can go.
We take for granted life's little things like being able to hear
and see to feel that biting wind upon our face or just simple
things like being able to tie your own shoelace.
Not being able to say the words must be really frustrating. Not
being able to understand must be like a curse.
What am I moaning about I can get up unaided for help I don't
need a nurse.
You know when I think of it life indeed can be a great deal
worse.

Aunt Jessica
Maureen Macnaughtan

Our dawn patrol was easy.
As the dominant years unfolded,
I took the short view

Stood on the same pier,
Followed her in every way
Never thought of another career.

To escape the back-streets
Instinct scrambled to the front.
She impressed walrus instructors
With her frail magnetism,
Even lived within her means
And wept for Sovietism.

Inspired by uncluttered beaches,
We marched without the gas-mask
Learned to drill and cart-wheels.
Her gang drank whisky-and-soda
Ladled soup and watched newsreels.

Marriage, the real preoccupation,
Made the differences cosmetic.
She manoeuvred bombers and fighters
All in the line of fire,
While we danced for tea
Somewhere in Lincolnshire.

Life As A Smoker
M A Govier

A little tear is forming
I feel like I could cry
ouch, it's stinging badly now
this smoke that's in my eye

you know that horrid feeling
the eye then goes all dry
you close it really slowly
to a threatening tear, and why?

I am puffing them old fags again
I really must be mad
I am furring up my innards
my sense of smell is bad

I choke and splutter daily
my smoke is everywhere
my adenoids are no good now
I puff yet just don't care

I'll cut my daily intake
from twenty down to ten
but now the weed has got me
it got me way back when

I thought I was the kiddie
but in fact was just a clown
because I'll be buried dirty
with lungs all thick and brown.

Haunted Castle
Leila M Manasseh

In Windsor, in the dead of night
Comforted with a fearsome sight
The frightened maid did promptly swoon
Beneath the shadow of the moon

What apparition did she see
Which terrified her utterly?
'Tis said the vision seems to weep
When mortals should be fast asleep
'Tis better not to leave one's bed
Than be encompassed with such dread
A warning to the faint of heart
If you don't wish to fall apart
And risk the terror and the fright
Don't venture from your room at night
Or better still keep far away
And only visit here by day.

Flight Of The Heart
Tracy Smith

The trees are but a whisper,
Over the beat that takes delight,
Watching the leaves sway mercilessly,
As the heart takes off in flight.

Spanning skies of threatening grey,
Whisking through the clouds,
Sauntering through the pelting rain,
The heart beats out aloud.

Searching for an awakening,
To clear the tormented sky,
The trees are stretching outward,
As the rain clouds pass on by.

Rainbows curve the airwaves,
Gntly smiling to all in sight,
A new leaf gently awakens,
As the heart beat ends its' flight.

Untitled
Martin Gareth Bayliss

Before I could move the bike had passed
With a 'whoosh!' and a clatter of stones;
Another followed, vanished 'round a turn.
Catching a 'hi-ya' on the wind, I smiled,
Strode on, putting the bike tracks behind me.
But further on a bike had been upturned:
The dark-haired boy sat crying at his knee,
His fair-haired mate softly patting his head,
Saying, "It happened to me as well."
His round, brown eyes wide in this sorrow,
He said to me, "It happened to me as well."
Rubbing his own head, "Just up there.
Near that gate over there." He waved his hand,
And upon it was an old white sock,
A funny but unsteady riding glove
Half of a pair he shared with his friend
- A joke they had, and by which I knew them.
It is a simple joy to love a child,
And in tears shed a beauty of feeling
More alive than any sensation.
And it is a great event to love
A stranger overturned by circumstance,
A child hurt by his own playfulness,
It is a thing endowing clarity
Through the warmth of selfless concern.

The Lough Drumbad
Jean McQuade

There were many families lived in Killee,
But my Uncle Jim's family were closest to me.
He part owned a lough, it was called Drumbad.
In the summer we fished for cream and cod.

From the tops of the hills you could see the lake
And the ripples on the water that the wind would make.
The sun shone down on the deep blue sheet
In the holidays, as it lapped around our bare feet.

It was set in the midst of fields and bog,
Where many's the time we walked Jim's dog,
And the glints on the water beckoned us over
To the beauty of Drumbad we'd daily discover.

Many's the picnic we had in its shade,
As we sat on the ditches and watched the sun fade.
It's hidden from many, known only to few,
The Lough Drumbad, a square mile or two.

Let's not dwell on memories past,
Or feast on nets that could be cast,
For looking back just makes me sad,
When I think of the days at Lough Drumbad.

A Final Thought
Michael A Packman

An old man slumps
On a forlorn beach
And weeps for a time
That no man knew.
His silken tears caress
The sand
Like the rising tide,
Which with temptation
Pulls the old mans heart
To beat within the surf.

Strangling, starving,
The harsh water
Forces the last breath
From the old man's chest
And his final tear
Burns deep into the
Naked flesh of the tide
Calling his memories
To the mountain top
He sits and blames the world.

Timetake
Ian Metcalfe

Take time

Make time

Buy time

Find time

Steal time

Give time

Before time takes you

I Waited
J A Taylor

"Leonard Norman Cohen,
Sing to me" she said,
From the desperate lonely heights
Of the gallery.
Our hearts were in our mouths,
Our hearts were finally broken,
With his words, so beautifully spoken.
He was singing for me, of course.
This pleading voice of death and destruction,
This voice of gold and of love
Echoed through the night, above
The gallery, where I was placed.

I waited at the door, but he did not come.
Leonard Norman Cohen,
Sing to me!

The Lady's Rune
David Orman

Death called, and I went willingly
Where others had not dared to tread;
My single purpose there to be
To arrest the dread of the place of the dead.

There I found what I sought not -
A love for all things beautiful,
That in the swirlings of all life
Rejuvenates the soul and blood.

What dies is born, what born must die,
Such is the rite of life itself;
A homage to the soul's innate
Desire and will to recreate.

The cauldron's secret so is given,
The potent potion's steadfast snare:
Into that cauldron we are driven
That from it life may reappear.

Alone
Dorothy Gould

When your loved one has gone
And you're left with your dreams

The loneliness surrounds you
Or so it seems

You sit in your chair
With your TV switched on
But you've no one to chat about
The programme that's on

But look around you and notice the joy
On the faces of a girl with a boy
Just think of the days together you shared
The moments you have treasured
And the moments you cared

You'll find being lonely is but a thought in your mind
Cast out that thought like a shadow and you'll surely find
Wherever you go or whatever you do
You're never alone your loved one's with you

To Our Old Black Labs, Bess And Teal
Heather Read

Empty places now
Where their heads used to bow
For me to kiss them goodnight
Before they would give me a paw
And settle down for the night
We shared happy times together
And enjoyed walks in all weather
No longer there to greet me each day
Or if I had been away
Wherever I go there are memories

Of places we walked and swam in the sea
As long as they were there I was strong
Now for our old black labs I long
With just their empty places now.

The Ultimate Ride
Ian Davies

From the valleys of the moon
to the dark mountains of shadow
I felt the need
the need to ride.
So I mounted a beast
a steed of insurmountable power
black as the panther
its wings shading the vile city
men and women cried
their children fled
as I passed far above.
We flew over many places
vast oceans, awesome mountains
all trembled beneath us.
Only when we reached the end
did my mount falter
yet I plunged on helplessly
tasting intertwined fear and ecstasy
knowing my inevitable conclusion
lay far, far beyond
within the cancerous vales of fire.

Boat Yard
Derek Frankland

A dramatic thrusting of masts skywards,
rigging threshing in the freshening breeze.

Brave hulls breasting from a streamlined knife-edge;
fibreglass smooth as steel, or old timbers
overlapped as clinker as a Viking.

But the keels are planted on the rough ground
and do not bite the unfurrowed river
that sweeps by so grey and unmolested,
so close I could spit in it if I cared.

Untitled
Phyllis Pearl

I awoke today and said a prayer
The morning looked real fair

The sunshine coming through the trees
Which landed on my window

A squirrel poised upon the lawn
The bird flying overhead to greet another morn!

The garden is a peaceful place
When you rise at dawn.

The Apple Tart
Kathleen Kernan

Today I'm baking,
It's a special treat,
Ingredients at their peak.
Oven at the ready,
Utensils spick and span,
It's time I began.

Sieving out the flour,
and letting in the air.
You know when I am baking
I just haven't got a care.
Just a little mix and lo
pastry comes together like this.

Freshly cooked apples,
golden pastry on the plate.
The aroma from my kitchen,
Would really touch your heart,
nothing could be simpler,
than to bake an apple tart.

Dream, Dream, Dream
Christine Griffiths

I dream of a house not far from here
With a special look of its own.
Not terraced or modern but semi-detached,
And would love it to be our home.

A driveway and trees, a large level lawn
Where children could safely play.
Borders of flowers with a fishpond cool,
And a path that surrounds them all.

French doors open onto a patio warm,
Where we could laze away happy hours,
On a summers morn.

Spacious rooms and sunny windows
Offer views that capture the eye,
And a door where one could stand
And gaze at a moonlit sky.

I visited this house four years ago
And long to be there again,
Whenever I'm out, I drive slowly past
And hope that my dream's not in vain.

Day-Dream
Margaret MacDonald

Drifting endlessly on waves of gold,
Pillowed on a cloud of white,
Now, poured into a yellow mould;
All earthly things drift from my sight.

Sun-kissed streams of light appear,
And silver stars and moons I see,
Up in a midnight sky so clear,
They flit and float, then disappear.

A magic city I see before me now,
Crystal domes and jewelled thrones,
No people there to greet and bow;
But breezes blow with softest moans.

A sapphire coach with horses lean,
Comes to take me home again,
I'm sad to leave, and yet I know
The beauty I saw was just a dream.

Strolling
Diane Wright

Look at me I'm strolling,
Proudly down the street,
All dressed up with a fancy hat,
With platforms on my feet.
The gentleman escorting me,
Is also very smart,
With a tail suit on and top hat,
A walking work of art.
The street it is so peaceful,
No people or cars in sight,
The sky is also very clear,
Not a bird circling in flight.
Just look at the lovely trees,
The leaves are turning gold,
Soon they will drop off and die,
Because they are too old.
Then there is the scenery,
Which makes my walk worthwhile,
It brings a sense of freedom,

Always making me smile,
Now I'm in reality,
Which isn't quite the same,
As I'm looking at a painting,
In a beautiful picture frame.

Carmine
Kate Sanders

Misty nights by the edge of cold, listless water.
A time when the restless are still and the still
Move
In eloquent silence amongst the rocks,
Forging their name in stone.
A time for Unknown to be king,
For Alone to have a companion,
For Silent to sing,
For Poor to touch riches.

Wretched water cannot glisten,
It dare not show its depth, only
Slowly lapping at those ghosts.
The water may take
Their memories to migrant shores,
But for this:
Cruel land hears not the unheard,
Yields not its treasures to the unrich,
Nor champions the solitary.
Our land thrusts,
Speaks,
And eats itself alive.

Unbidden Memories
T L Grandi

Go for a walk to be alone,
too much sadness,
Put on my coat, go out ungloved,
they remind me of someone,
Someone I loved.

Autumn leaves stir under my feet
faded and crumpled, sad to see,
fresh wind blowing on my face,
reminds me, I quicken my Pace.

Hair whipping around my head
as clouds gather in the sky,
Coat wrapped tighter, against the cold
reminds me, that I'm getting old.

Feel something wet and cold and on my face,
White stuff falling all around
Pretty snowflakes, melt on the ground,
Start to settle on an old iron gate,
reminds me, to stop and appreciate.

Wyatt Earp's Budgie
Jeff Wiseman

Will an eskimo shiver on warm sunny nights?
Did Gungha Din's mother play trumpet?
And if you give sugar to buzzards in flight,
Are they likely to like it or lump it?

Is a lumberjack's shirt always checked for the dirt?
Is a train driver's job up for tender?
And is a coquette really French for a flirt?
Or does it depend on the gender?

Was Lamburgher Gessler, itinerant wrestler,
The cause of the Austrian fair boom?
And is there a barber in Scarborough Harbour
Who weaves brand new wigs on his hairloom?

If you tumble in spring are you hurt by the fall?
Will an owl ever suffer from daymares?
Does a funeral director's job threaten to pall?
And do black and white snobs put on grey airs?

Did Einstein's pet whippet run rings round his eyes?
Did Sergeant conduct without baton?
Was Listz ever kissed by a woman the size
Of King Kong, stood up straight, with his hat on?

Was Shakespeare's first name not William, but Jim?
Did Bunsen invent the first burner?
Could Wyatt Earp's budgie burp louder than him?
And did Ivy once climb Annapurna?

O.A.P.
Margaret Lewis

"We'd like a bungalow," we said
When we get old and slow,
Then, why oh why, do I feel so sad
Now it's time for us to go.

We don't like it to be known
That we are on a pension.
We'd much sooner hide the fact
Not bring it to attention.

So, I think we'll plod along
For another year or so.
Doing the things we've always done
'Till it's time for us to go.

Untitled
C North

Soft music from the waterfall
Plays gently in my head
As I'm walking by the river
Bringing lightness to my tread

The water is an orchestra
Playing Natures instruments
Conducted by the seasons
And I'm the audience

Summer is the dreamy flow
Soft as the violin
Caressed by loving fingers
Bringing happiness within

Autumn speeds the tempo
With trumpet's sighing breeze
Playing through the rushes
At the waters edge with ease

The harsher clash of cymbals
Signal Winter's on it's way
Muddying the riverbed
and clouding up the day

The triangle and xylophone
Tinkle over rocks and wiers
The beauty of the dawning Spring
is music to my ears

Don't Tell
Phyllis Audrey Callow

The fairies say I must not tell
How old I am today
I only know I feel so young
as youth in every way.

My hair though dyed is really grey
Or white - I do not know,
I've tried to be most careful
Yet my eyes have lost their glow.

But inner beauty stays with me
From which I'll never part
And warmth and love is with me
And wrapped around my heart.

For what is age and calendar
A time that passes by
With life and much experience
Sometimes you laugh or cry.

And so the 'Fairies' call again
As every year they say
Just keep the world a-guessing
"How old you are today."

Egg Sandwiches
Lesley J Freeman

A heat haze mirage shimmered on the molten motorway,
the glinting chrome of static cars stretched endlessly away.

Perspiring vinyl overcame the airless window's plea,
I pushed aside the nausea and the comics from my knee.

As though my prayers were answered it appeared that we were
there,
I unfolded from my stifling cocoon and gulped the air.

The heavy scent of new mown grass rose sweetly from the
farms,
the August sun glared hotly on my rucksack and my arms.

Our stumbling boots ascending moorland stones made
progress slow,
but soon the glistening reservoirs stretched out like glass
below.

A purple, patchwork heather cloaked each undulating hill,
hypnotically patrolled by bees, each buzzing for its fill.

A warm breeze rippled waves across the gorse and bracken
sea,
a grazing sheep moved on and sent a rabbit darting free.

Through lichen crusted rocks a glittering stream danced on its
way,
its bubbling crystal depths enticing damsel flies to play.

I flopped down in the long, coarse grass and grazed up at the
sky,
deep blue with wisps of cotton wool, a skylark circled high.

I closed my eyes and listened to the stream and distant sheep,
tranquility washed over me, I drifted into sleep.

My reverie was halted by the "Picnic's ready!" call,
then rolling to my side, with great delight, I saw it all...

A perfect summer setting, my contentment was complete,
all this, and now it seemed we had egg sandwiches to eat!

For My Father
Samantha Wood

The world is always changing,
And perhaps it seems to you,
The values that you taught me,
Are the ones that I outgrew.

In many ways we're not alike,
But daddy, can't you see?
The things I learnt from you
Are what I value most in me.

Waiting
Charles Harris

Platform
Shoes,
60's
Minutes
Late the train

Again, I am waiting.
It seems that all my life
I am cramped in trains
Of thoughts, between this and that resort,
A subtle retort, that, foolish perhaps,
But only the punctual will succeed,
Whilst others feed from lines
Running
Parallel,
But never quite touching, you understand;
They always have the upper hand
Gesturing first-class expletives,
Deleted only in polite conversation,
Round silver spoons in fashionable stations,
Announcing: Engagements, estrangements,
Things running on time
Tables of mahogany, so polished,
That you can see working-class faces shine,
Politely asking: "Is the train on time?"

Dreamer
Janette Ross

Flying boats, heavy liners
struggling swishing
criss cross ropes.
Breaking free, she reaches up
as the sky thunders,
with trembling clouds.
But I know that
boats can't fly!
Philadelphia paddles high.
My heart is pounding,
waiting, watching.
My blood runs cold
for her bow is broken!
Suddenly she spews the people,
arms, legs and screaming heads.
All around confusion splutters,
snapping, cracking, breaking bones.
Watches, purses, bows and buttons,
teeth and diamonds fall from heaven.
A shower of flying, crying people.
I try to run these feet are lead!
the darkness grows,
am I dead?

The Silent Partner
Heather Whittaker

There is a silence now where once you were,
There is a hush, a calm without a stir.

There is a chill, great numbness in my heart.
Such disbelief, that we could ever part.

There is a passion, breathing in my soul,
It sighs alone, created by the hole,
That once you filled, so deep and to the brim;
The shame of living, batters me within.

They laid down flowers, a monument in life,
Each tiny petal, a twisting of the knife.
Young men die young, yes those whom God loves most,
Young men die fast, Father, Son and Holy Ghost.

September Trees
Edward Tanguy

So fled the afternoon,
for apples were violet.
We entered the forest, dreamed by our past,
now surrounded by yearling Rivers of Wine.
Hold,
do not look towards pink oceans
or your fish are rope.
Anytime you are walking use
different eyes.
Eyes are looking from plant to rock,
Eyes from the ground pushing
you into the next viking cloak.
Small birds with electric shadows
dance your name in garnets.
Mind your intellect, some
houses are not inquiring, only a mystics

purse is vandalised.
Egyptian Roses flame your hand;
nearly there,
a sabre of light shafts the pines, a flutter
of dark wings and we are out of the mauve night.

Enchanted Child
Zoey Dempsey

Golden hair flying,
Twirling round and round,
The enchanted child
Dances to the bottom of the garden.
There the willows whisper
And the fairies dance with the daisies.

Eyes bright,
She spies a flower,
Deep, purple, wild as the wind.
Stopping down to pluck the flower,
She stumbles and falls,
Into the calm still brook.

The child struggles,
But the evil depths,
Have her in their clutch.
Pain in her eyes,
Fear in her heart,
Her body falls into the blackness of the brook.

Her soul is kept though,
Captured by the enchantment of the garden.

She is still seen now,
Dancing, twirling, golden hair flying,
But now she is a fairy,
Dancing in the garden.

My Heart
J Kattenburg

My heart is but a gaping wound
Where blood pours instead of trickles;
Not just cracked, not merely broken
But pulled apart, violently,
Stretched as by traction,
Forced to excrete its life juice
And allow it to pour freely weeping
Over all the essential organs that need to stay dry
Compact and airtight

My heart is but a cancerous division
Of overgrown cells and unnatural growths,
Divided into monstrous chambers,
Scarred by the tracks of congealed blood,
Constantly reopened and reformed

My heart is but a series of fragments
Lacerated by cut crystal glass
Pierced by every broken segment
Sparkling and gleaming on immaculate floors

In Memory Of Donald
H North

Oh Donald dear,
I can see you here,
Sitting in your favourite chair.
You wave to me as I pass by,
And carry on my way,
One eye on the telly
The other on the drive.
Hoping to see a visitor,
Popping in to see,
How you are getting on,
Over a cup of tea.

Now the chair is empty
But I still remember you
Looking up at me and smiling
From your favourite chair.

I still look after the garden
And tend it with loving care.
But it seems only yesterday
That you were sitting there.
God Bless.

Shadows
Joan Milbourne

Meet me by the tower, 'neath the night time's sky
Where moonlight casts it's shadows over the moor.
Whisper that you love me and for love you'd surely die
Tell me now, I silently implore.

Meet me by the old oak, in the twilight sun,
Where shadows cast their silent shapes so dire.
Convince me that you need me and your life has just
begun
Tell me now, to set my heart on fire.

Meet me by the lamplight, in the market square,
Where two shadows can become entwined as one.
Promise now to stay with me, forever to be there,
Then I will know that my life has begun.

1993

Hazel McKendrick

It says in the Bible
That Man will fight man
An' nation wae nation
So it wisnae faur wrang
As trouble the noo
Did no seem tae cease
Whitever his happened
tae whit we ca'ed peace
If they ca' pit a stop tae a' this harange
It's meast likely the world
Will gan up wae a bang
In the worst o' they times
We should ayeweys hiv hope
But try no tae get it
Frae stuff we ca' Dope

Watt Power
M Bell

What power beyond yon concrete lies
blowing white spiral sighs, into a blood red sky.

Slotted neatly beyond yon rock, the power's
contained within a building block.
Reactors cool down into a silver foaming sea, for
energy, that's progress made, this century.

The fish like it hot in that particular spot.
The bird life is fine, just to dine, is devine,
for the 'Anglers' and Twitchers in their spare time.
With smiles that say, the pleasures all mine,
we are feeling so sublime.

The Sombre Somme
Stephen Loney

Through Hell's Gateway passed a generation
Fighting for the good of the Nation
How good it was of Hague to say
Walk slow and proud and enjoy the day.

In a matter of minutes the guns had quenched
Their thirst for death in the mud and stench
Young men in their prime lay dead and gone
Victims of the infamous Somme.

The shining sun now masked by shell smoke
Those yet to die thinking of their home folk

Enthusiasm replaced by sheer disbelief
From the German barrage came no relief.

The folly of it all is beyond compare
If only more lives this battle could spare
Every town and hamlet in the onlooking nation
Could not envisage Hell's creation.

Sombre Somme you're undying shame
Has swallowed up name after name
Each in their prime, so much left to give
Memories with which we have to live.

With deep regret some 80 years on
We still recall the horrors of the Somme
Not for their greatness, but for their will to entice
Young men to the abominable sacrifice.

An Easier Way
Abina Russell

Ten black eyes stared at me,
five yellow beaks opened
as I peeped in the privet hedge
at their home of mud and straw.

I had known them before,
as blue green eggs with brown
markings, laid by mother
blackbird, with a loud screech.

She sat the eggs; left only
for meals - when I saw the shells crack
and split open, big heads all beak
and eyes and small bodies emerged.

She fed them on slugs and worms,
until brown/black feathers grew,
and the nest grew too small; one sat
on the edge, one overhead.

One dawn I heard twittering,
flapping of wings, rustling in
the privet as the fledglings
hopped out to find their wings.

Night fell, a sudden silence spread;
I peeped into the nest, empty all had
fled; only mud and straw, she too
flew free until next year.

True Friends
G M Rowland

We fill the air with poisoned gases
We scorch the land with burning oil,
Polluting air, polluting water,
All lifes gifts we seem to spoil.

We must stop our bouts of madness,
The earth is not ours by birth.
Paradise could be ours if we protect her,
Tomorrow could be heaven on earth.

We know the earth won't last forever,
We are tearing it all apart.
Let's protect our children's future,
Everyone must play their part.

Come on! Let's work together,
Send this message to your heart.
Insure a future for your children,
Be a 'True Friend' to the earth.

Reflections
Frances Fox

If I could walk beside myself
I wonder what I'd see;
a child perhaps, lost and alone
or a woman of destiny.

If I could walk beside myself
would I help me along lifes way,
or would I watch me stumble
and also lose my way;

If I could walk beside myself
would I like what I could see,
or would I want to turn me out
and make another me.

If I could walk beside myself
along this journey climb through life,
would the journey be any easier,
would there be less sign of strife.

If I could walk together
mind, body, soul as one;
would I be at peace
when my journey's finally run.

How To Stample
Shirley Soutar

First, unbutton the button
Unzip the zip.
Then wriggle the trousers
down over your hips.
Put one foot on the bottom,
no, don't turn round
Skin tight jeans
won't just fall to the ground.
Pull your foot from the leghole
But oh! it's too tight
You'll fall flat on your face
if you don't do this right.
The next step is really a tricky manoeuvre
You'll probably have to do it twice over.
Stand on the legs while extracting the feet
Eventually you will be stood in the seat.
The visual effects will take laughter to tears
Not trampling, or stamping
But stampling, my dears.

Hair-Ache
David Willoughby

In the mirror she would stare
Cursing at her 'Afro' hair.
It's too frizzy, and too thick
All this hair, it makes me sick.
Why can't mine be long and straight
Like my friend at school called Kate.
I always need my Mum to brush it
It hurts my head when she has to rush it.
Pulled back and tied, or sometimes plaited
However it's done, it still gets matted.
How I wish my hair was straight
Like my friend at school called Kate.
Off to face another day at school
"Is my hair all right, I feel a fool"
Mum drops me off near the school gate
Who should I see, but my friend Kate.
"Hello Emma, I think that we're early
I like your hair, I wish mine was curly".

Arab Horses At Winestead
Dennis Dee

Grey and stately stands the hall, amid the trees at
Winestead.
Shades of splendour there still linger, of a life that once
was led,
Cedar trees, and lovely parkland, shrouded in a misty
dawn,
Summer dresses, joy and laughter, parties on the tennis

lawn.
Arched the pillars in the stables, aromas in the
saddleroom,
Of leather cleaning, medication, and the pipe smoke of
the groom.
Arabian horses, equine beauty, all of famous
"Crabbet-blood",
Loved by Kings, and eastern rulers, from some distant
desert stud.
Mares and foals content at Winestead grazing on historic
sward,
Destined to be someone's treasure, in the country and
abroad.
The years roll by, and much has gone, but through a
ghostly haze,
Come forms of silent men and horses from those lost
"Elysian days".
Perfect motion, grace and presence, descendants of a
summer clime,
The Creator made him for mans pleasure, Hoof-prints in
the sands of time.

It's A Hard Life
Robert Simpson

I wake up freezing on a summer's day
Life is hard even though I'm made for play
It's cramped and tight where I reside
With my brother Bill pressed against my side
We're moving now and will soon be free
The strength of the sun makes it hard to see
Able to breathe, my fur keeping me hot

Starting to move to a different spot
But wait, what's this, I'm being squeezed
My body distorts and doesn't feel well pleased
Worse is to come as I am to discover
A ferocious blow nearly removes my cover
With blinding speed causing a terrific pain
My head is spinning as I'm hit again and again
There's no relief from this treatment so hard
My body's bruised, my fur's all scarred
Suddenly it's quiet, and I roll to a stop
No longer able to jump so high or hop
Back into my box I'm thrust with mere disdain
To be left in the dark until required again
It's difficult to accept that my career is now downhill
But life can be harsh when all is still
This is not a career that I can recommend
Being a tennis ball is no fun when you reach the end.

Evening
C D Casstles

Reclined in the lazy-boy chair,
Brown eyes closed,
I watch your face...
Gentle in repose...
Motionless.
Breathing stirs
The mystic silence
As Summer's bright
Discerning gaze
Fails, drifting into a
Dusty drowsiness...

Dusk filters through
French doors
Hinged on twilight;
Dark hair shades to grey
Harsh lines fade;
Walls melt, merge
With outer space
Where heaven is a
Quiet place;
Universal love,
And ours...
The warmth of home.

Rhymes
Steve Sheppard

Your poems don't rhyme they complained -
But they do -

They rhyme for the sea as she sighs on the sand
They rhyme for the leaves that are green
They rhyme for the lover who weeps for his lass
That rhyme for the rhymes unseen

They rhyme for the seasons - the wind and the snow
They rhyme for the stars and the sun
And in the hearts of men yet unborn
So shall they rhyme when I am gone.

Death-Bed Portrait
L M Calvey

This man had thought of sweet Ophelia
Then painted regal death in shades decreed
by imperious she who, dead, lay beneath the ambered orb
of earlier death she could not rule without. Little relict, and
her memento mori;
His stately form so black and stern. And she like Botticelli
parted
Webbed in veils of winding cloths like foaming water, like the
earth's first froth -
It is a sweet and self-engendering splendour,
This view of death that died with old Victoria.

How they loved this power lying in death, those
who wore the crown and wield the brush, the pen.
Did Shakespeare view his girl so soft, so purely
smothered in this purple gauze, this glaze of flowery water? If
not,
Where did it all begin?

The Queen. Ophelia. Little Elizabeth at Carisbrooke,
And unknown others, still-limned in marble, smoothed
by oddly nuptial falls of pall and stream and stone
Where flowers lie plucked, their colour bleaching
like the blood of those whose final forms they soothe.

A fashion's died at Osborne with the Queen.
The tributes ache no more with tremulous and frozen pity,
and woman's image is no longer rosebud, lilly, violet.
This regal homage flowing in romantic folds - its time
Has passed, and there's a stronger garment now,
Rising from the self.

But still death stalks her, and there's acid in his line.

To A Russian Sailor
Anna Parker-Rees

Cape Town, July 1993

You came from afar
To die in an unknown land,
To lie in your blood like Christ
Till the sunrise.

In the hour of prayer
Bullets flew, spitting hate.
Let us pray, though it is too late;
Let us learn to share

For nothing is fair
In this life except knowing
We die in Christ.

But before the harvest the sowing
before the dying the fight
Before the darkness the light.

Promise
S N Crocker

As in a dream,
You caught my small child's hand
And held it in a scream.

Wrenched my hands, clinging,
from my frozen face

And let me fall,
Deep, into that feared, forbidden place.

Yet as in a dream,
Through my fear I sensed your warmth,
Soft feather floating sound
Bearing me gently to the ground
Breathing promise, I would not break,
After the storm, had left the dream
Shattered in its' wake.

Passing Thoughts
Stanley Bates

How golden the future when we are young,
So many promises and things to be done.
We set our hopes and dreams on high,
We don't always win but we give it a try.
The book of life with its empty pages,
Waits to be filled as we go through the ages.
The years will pass by and we will grow old,
With age comes wisdom so we are told.
The boldness of youth is replaced by caring,
Thinking of others and troubles sharing.
We recall the past with its chances missed,
When things turned out not quite as we wished.
We remember the good times also the bad,
The times we were happy the times we were sad.
The years gone by are over and past,
But our special memories will ever last.
We face the future young or old,
Living a life more precious than gold.

Lifes race is on so we do our best,
When the runnings over then we may rest.
Get in the race and make a good start,
Remember in life we all have a part.
Life can play tricks so just bear in mind,
Try to be caring above all be kind.

Little Orphan
S Cook

I'm just a little orphan from the war.
My mummy and daddy are here no more.
I lost my little sister and my little brother too,
And now I'm all alone and don't know what to do.
I'm just a little orphan and I'm so hungry
And so tired.
I'm lost and lonely and just sit here and cry.
Can only see the sky
Can't see the houses
And when I turn my head
Can only see people lying there - dead.
I'm just a poor little orphan.
I heard the bombs and bullets
When they hit the wall.

My daddy died last night.
My mummy was dead three days ago
My brother and sister this morning died
Now all I've done is sit here and cried.
I think that all that I can do,
Is just to wait to join them
When I die too.

Motorway Madness
Elizabeth Spencer

Six o'clock in the morning
And the weary drivers
Blinking away the fog of sleep,
Pour relentlessly bumper upon bumper,
Lights blinding, flashing, horns sounding
Lane changing, to work.

The throbbing of the radio's cacophony
Paces them, as blinded by their thoughts
They drive seeing yet unseeing.
Their only care - their own ultimate destination.

A yellow, sulphuric pall shrouding the motorway
Goes unnoticed until in a moment of panic
The lorry driver slams on his brakes,
Jacknifes.

And catapulting vehicles zigzag
Driving too fast, too close,
Careering hither and thither
With wild abandon.

The air is filled with the screaming
Of metal wrenched;
Of bodies broken, burnt, maimed,
Dead.

Motorway madness once more
Has collected its toll.

Pollution
Lara Dalby

Pollution, pollution, it's everywhere,
It's here and it's over there.
It's in rivers and in the sea,
Next thing you know it'll be in you and me.
You don't realise that it's there,
You breathe it in because it's in the air.
It can get into the darkest corner on earth,
But the earth is more than what it's worth;
We've got to stop pollution before it's too late,
We'll all soon die at this rate.

Untitled
Andrea Marks

The little boy looked, and with a big sigh,
tried a weak smile and hold his head high.
He'd wanted to go for a long time there,
to be too young was not at all fair.
He wanted to spend the day with his Dad,
after all, he had a sister, but he was the lad.
He just wanted line, a hook and some bait...
if they went quite early they wouldn't be late.
But Dad said "No, come with me next time
The tide will be better for more fish on the line".
One little tear escaped from his eye,
as he turned to his Dad to whisper "Goodbye".
Dad looked at his face, then changed his mind,
"Oh, come on then, let's see what we find".
Mum wrapped him up warm and gave them a snack,

warning them not to be too late back.
It was a great day, but no fish to bring home.
The best for Son was to have Dad on his own.

Someone New
Kathryn Russell

Someone's come to live with us
He's tiny pink and new
His face is rather crinkled up
His hands are crinkly too

His eyes can hardly open
I think they must be stuck
His mouth is open all the time
To cry a lot or suck

If I put my finger
In one of his small hands
He holds it very tightly
So I think he understands

How long I waited for him
And how glad I am he came
Cause he's my baby brother
And Adam is his name

The Things I Love
Dorothy Mewett

I love to see the birds at dawn,
The sweetest smell of a new mown lawn.
These are the things I love.

I love to see a face of bliss,
Two sweetest lips to place a kiss.
The simple things I love.

I love all flowers that come my way,
The sight of the harvester making the hay.
God sent us these things for us to love.

I love the dew on a summers morn
or the frozen earth with its secrets unborn.
These are all free for us to love.

So kneel and praise the lord with me
and thank him for his beauty free.
Two eyes are all we need to see,
The beauty that he loves.

The Garden Year
Anouska Aitkenhead

January brings the snow,
makes our feet and finger glow.
February brings the rain,
thaws the frozen lakes again.
March brings breezes, loud and shill,

to stir the dancing daffodils.
April brings the primrose sweet,
scatter daisies at our feet.
May brings flocks of pretty lambs,
skipping by their fleecy dams.
June brings tulips, lilies, roses,
fill the childrens hands with posies.
July brings cooling showers,
apricots and gilly flowers.
August brings the sheaves of corn,
then the harvest home is borne.
September brings the fruit,
then sports men begin to shoot.
October brings the pheasant,
then to gather nuts is pleasant.
November brings the blast,
Then the leaves are wriling fast.
December brings the sleet,
blazing fire, a Christmas treat.

Going To The Theatre
C Higgins

One evening with nothing better to do
To the theatre I thought I would go.
I had no idea of what it entailed
Or what they intended to show

Would it be musical, comedy, farce
Would it be sad or funny?
Would I forget the world outside,
Would it be worth the money?

I sat enthralled throughout the first half
The cast was very well chosen.
The timing was good, lines well rehearsed,
And players all kept their clothes on!

The interval started, the curtain came down
The refreshments included ice cream.
With tea and coffee served in the lounge
You could even have scone, jam and cream.

Interval over, the curtains went up
As I sat in my seat once again.
The second half was as good as the first.
I think I'll go there again.

Child Of Flies
Peter Wilton

Child of flies,
all you have to eat.
I resist the urge to look away,
and watch your tongue loll
your eyes glaze.

No one changes
your dirty sheets,
but would it stop
the mosquitoes biting,
the dust settling,
your stomach from gnawing
only bullets and gunfire.

I don't feed you.
I don't comfort.
You are an impulse on the screen.
I will never meet you.
You are a dead world away.

This first-world father;
persecutor,
oppressor,
camera,
is still watching.

The Yobbo's Lament
Martin Wilkinson

A nayber tryd to burn my tree, to burn it to the grownd,
My wyf went red "yu tell im Fred", she sed, so I went rownd,
I shouted an' I swar at 'im, I didn't 'arf rant and rave.
I fretened, darnsed and waved my hands, cor, I wernt 'arf
brave!
"I'll hang one on yer if yer burn my tree agayn, I'll bash yer",
I jumped and cryd,
My nayber larfed and larfed so much I fort he wood have
dyed,
'Cos wot I didn't no wos it had been an axident,
The wind cort the flames of his barbeeq, the wind had turnd
and bent,
So now I feel a rite pratt having acted lyk a yob,
Nex tym I'll be moor careful, I'll lern to shut my gob.
Now yu myt wunder wy I feel for that tree, wy I fink of it
such a lot,
Wy, so wood yu if yu wer lyk me - it's the only home I'v got!

Thoughts On A Mining Village
Yvette Ayers

Miners cottages stand on the hill
Back to back and moaning still
About their paintwork which
Is now turned black.
Chimneys bellow out the smoke
Whilst below the houses choke
And the doctor tends another Asthma attack.
Clouds leave the sky cold and pale
The sun long since left this vale
Retreating from an enemy of smog and grime
White surrender flags tainted grey
Herald another washing day
Waste of yet more dark and blackened time.

Unborn
Pamela McCaughey

Today you kicked so definitely
In the place where she kicked
Today you slept so serenely under a heart weeping
In the place where she slept
And my heart paused to listen to the bleating of yours
Bleating and beating
In that intimate place that belonged to her
And to you
And to me
Where she lived and breathed
And stopped living
Where you breathe
Today I gave you my world.

Today you lay so poignantly
On the side where she lay to die
And out of pain like concrete burning
Curled comfort around something cold
And life's blood whispered feverishly
In the veins
Please don't die where she died
For you no more belong in the ground
Than she does
Where pretty petals sway
In the sacred intimacy of shared roots
In a tenderness that knows no trust.

Squabbling
Jonathan Beck

Over half moon glasses
The will is read
The damage is done
The word is said
Gasps, smiles, tears
He spoke so mournfully
After all I did for you
Keep it in the family.

50 years hard labour
Split up in seconds
His name was hardly mentioned
A new existence beckons,
Can't let him get in the way
The solicitor gets his percent
Not from this blood line
Our money most hastily spent.

Reflections
G E Coates

We were here before the pill,
A pill, we took if we were ill.

Time sharing meant togetherness,
Dressing up, more clothes not less.

We wore silk stockings, hitched with suspenders
before panti hose became contenders.

Young people then, did not wear Jeans.
Aids were treatments for beauty queens,

Girls wore peter pan collars, yes they did,
and thought cleavage was something the butcher did.

Grand buildings were never called carbuncles,
and going to a 'porn' shop, meant going to uncles.

Pot was a utensil complete with a lid on,
Female personals were something to be hidden.

Grass was for mowing, should you feel hale and hearty,
a gay person meant only, life and soul of the party.

Many are the changes we have had to survive,
Yet I am so glad at being alive.

In these turbulent times Nineteen Ninety Three,
No longer called an O.A.P.
A senior citizen that's me.

Summer
Roy Cummings

Summer time is here at last
Winter chills have now long past,
The soaring swallow will arrive
While bumble bee is making hive.

Meadow's yield their ripening hay
As in the breeze the treetops sway,
Golden barley in their ears
Await the noise of combine shears.

The swift soars from sea to downs
As kestrel hovers above the towns,
Beaches thronged in golden sands
Full of children with their demands.

The meadow flowers await the rain
To quench away their thirsting pain,
As rainfall, is quickly spent
The flower's respond with perfumed scent.

At last the rain has now passed by
Birds of song fill the sky,
The seagulls scour the golden sand
As coloured blossom marks the land.

Life's A Carousel
P J Jackson

The childs' tears burst like a balloon
that he holds in his hand
The madman fears the harvest moon
but doesn't understand
The blindman looks but cannot see
beyond his darkened cell
Circumstance goes round and round
and life's a carousel.

The ocean tide shall rise and sweep
and turn away again
Clouds will hide and softly sleep
until it's time to rain
Gravestones crack and shiver
with the tolling of the bell
That rings of Sunday morning birth
for life's a carousel.

An old love dies a sudden death
when the thrill is passed and lost
A new love sighs a fresher breath
a kiss is all it costs
As the petals of a true loves bloom
all wither where they fell
Love shall cast a new-sown seed
for life's a carousel.

Puddledub
Margaret McDougall

She said she came from 'Puddledub'
as he danced with her that night.
He never asked where Puddledub was
Suspecting he was right
In thinking she was being smart
when answering him that night.

A lovely girl he'd thought she was
when first they'd waltzed that night.
Her eyes were blue as a child-painted sky,
Her eyes so warm he might
Have asked if they could meet again
Had her answer just been right.

No more did he think of the girl he'd met
at the dance, 'til later in life,
An old man driving along a country road
One evening, with his wife,
Saw a signpost, an arm outstretched
saying 'Puddledub' - somewhere in Fife.

Birth
Beryl Thompson

New life unfolds, giving birth
to wants and whims and love.
First born, your welcome child
has given birth to parent-hood.
Gentle caring, joy in sharing
laughter, tears... and constant love.

Running Scared
Shealagh Crabb

This bloody road remains a mystery
the path which we travel is never ending
is it of our expectations?
Does it hold the great mixture of life
compared with nature - will we ever know, or
only accept there is a path to be followed until
our destination is reached.
Will we ever attain the new brighter meaning of life
will it become clear, allowing us to understand,
with empathy the plight of others
who knows the final outcome - who would know?
would the supplication of knowledge allow us to
become better people?
probably not?
is this the true meaning of living,
ambition, greed, war,
we simply cannot be at peace with the world,
the living creatures of nature know calm,
peace and grace - yet,
we do not follow
why? why?
the human race will never win, nor
will it ever end
we are simply running scared.

Vulnerable Tonight
Kristina Moore

Please don't frighten me, I'm vulnerable tonight.
My ghosts are unsettled;
I feel them shifting in my mind like moths wings,
and a shiver of unease runs through me.
I don't know why, words can't explain.

The room around us is cosy,
firelight lapping at the walls, dappling the ceiling.
I look to the flames for comfort, but
they mock me, dancing into pictures and scenes
I shudder to see.

You sit opposite me across the table,
tracing your own secret life in the fire.
There is something wild about you tonight,
something questing, searching,
your soul reaching out to places you could never
describe,
riding on a dark unknown wind.
Another night I would fly with you,
exhilarating in the strangeness, the darkness,
the side of your spirit the world can't see.
But tonight I am afraid.
In your hands, your face, your eyes, I sense
that you have gone on alone,
and the gentleness and understanding I crave
has left with you.

Don't hurt me, darling. I'm vulnerable tonight.

Untitled
A Summers

Have you ever stopped to watch
A child at play and unaware,
That anyone is in the room, -
That anyone is there.
The concentration on it's face.
The way it moves it's hands
The way it learns which bit fits which,
As it slowly understands.
The sadness when a toy is 'broke',
The glee at playing tricks.
The temper when a part gets stuck,
And laughter when it's fixed.
They learn so much, these little ones,
But they teach us something, too.
To quietly sit and watch a child,
Is a rewarding thing to do.

What's A Perfect Day
Jean Griffin

To wake up to the song of the birds
The hum of a bee
No clock watching
Have a lazy breakfast
The quick dash to the shower
replaced by the soak in the bath

A time to read the book
You never finished

Do things you like to do
My perfect day starts tomorrow
So why am I wondering what to do?

July 1990, Kuwait
Margaret Anne Foreman

When you are older than you are today
And time has stolen your hopes away
But left the present, and your memories
Remember your youth and remember me
And a summer of simple, enchanting joy
Wrought by your youth and a gentle boy
Whose eyes were as warm as the summer rain.

Can you picture his face again?
Or have you forgotten, as time goes by
His innocent love? And here you sigh
You think of a war and remember a face
For he carried yours, and died for your race.
But stop, don't wake from your reverie
Remember our summer, remembering me.

Mourning Expression
Angela Williams

My mind is never satisfied
However much it's fed,
And when my thoughts are unified
I have an aching head,
I feel the pain that lives inside

A heart of heavy lead;
'Though I am torn and I have cried
And wish that I were dead,
I do the thing that's dignified
And write a rhyme instead.

Conflict
Susan Bevin

Compassion, why don't you rule us alone?
Perhaps the intellect, knowing the course
To our final maze of torturing moan
Finds our mistakes to be the sorrow's source
And learning this, cannot blind seeing eyes
But must whip out the tongue lashing our wounds
And turn again the wheel with words wise
Mimicking the cries wrenched from writhing moods
Or perhaps, chooses to add to the gifts
Of your rosy smiles, its frowns of thorns
And bloodies your leaves as it scratching sifts
Our heart's core, unveiled scarred, scorching thoughts
But, when you are moved, such is your power
The intellect's scorn can only cower.

Untitled
Peggy Jones

Who is the old woman with her shopping
Climbing so painfully up the steep hill,
Cars chugging upward, passing, not stopping,
But, hopefully some day, one of them will.

Nearly bent double in her coat of red,
Hem low at the front, and high at the back,
With bright woolly cap pulled down on her head
Clutching the shopping bag, bulging and black.
When she arrives at her home on the hill,
With bone weary legs, and spine fit to crack,
I truly hope that there is someone still
Waiting to love her and welcome her back.

If Only
Anita Aplin

If Only, just two simple words
We took time to listen to the birds,
To see the flowers in full bloom
Instead of going round in gloom.

If Only, we could help each other more
The world would be better for sure,
The tensions would all disappear,
Then perhaps we could live without fear.

If Only, things were not out of reach
Perhaps our children we could teach,
Love, happiness and peace of mind
Which we have found so hard to find.

If Only, it is so easy to say
But usually too late in the day,
Now we are on our own and lonely
Because of those two words, If Only.

Royull Simpafizz
David Asgrove

Ar do simpafize wiv them Royulls
thair ployt just brings tears t' me oyz
ar feel duty bairnd t' send munny
or sum uther tax free supprize
un tho ar kips in a box near th' Bull Ring
it ay code that keeps me up all noyt
but worrying' fa' Charls un Diana
'ave thay eaten, is Fairgy all royt

It ay wair oyll nick me sum grub from
that giz me a raison t' fret
ar do care abairt mass unemplymunt
after all, non ov them ay wairked yet
no, arm more consairned wi' thair welfair
ar need to no that them okay
admittidley, thay war electid
but dimocrissy wairks that way

An arm wurried abowt the Royull 'ousold
Winza Cassull, it went up in smowk
tho it war till they menshunned rebildin' costs
tha' I 'eard it belungs to us foke
but ar doo simpafize wiv them Royulls
tho arm beat by thair confidunse trick
thay must stair inta spays whilst tairnin' thair fayse
from the ungry the omeliss un sick

Yess ar do simpafize wiv them Royulls
thair puzishun qweschunned at last
can th' still be a playce
in ar strugglin rayce
or doo thay belung t' th' passt

Is It Right
Samantha Boasman

The animals are kept shut away
With unneeded clothes and make up.
The box office tickets sell out fast
People pay to see unhappy animals.
When the show is over
The poor lonely souls are pushed
into cold damp cell.
In the morning the sun rises
But still no escape
Is it right.

The Unknown Soldier
Jackie Hodson

"Ten pence for some tea love?"
Is it too much to ask?
Only a few surrender,
Digging deep for change that
Won't be missed.
Not enough care,
The sight is all too familiar.
Shuffling along, so lonely
In worn out rags.
We turn away, disgusted
By the smell of neglect.
Another tramp, nobody wants to know
The soldier who fought,
once so proud and brave.
Now begging the meagre comfort

Of warmth and conversation.
He almost lost his life for us,
Do we care now?
"Ten pence for some tea love?"
Is it too much to ask?

Web Of Destruction
Jayne Cole

How often do we catch our wings in a spider's web,
Not realising the danger upon which we tread,
Putting our trust in synthetics,
Destroying all morals and ethics.

Just like a butterfly we flutter around,
Brilliant colours adorning our bodies,
Until our minds are sucked dry by every tempting
sigh and sound.

Some coping, others unable to face solidarity,
Seek a solution of floating on air,
Through pills and injections, often successful
suicide.

To keep clear of such magnetism is happiness indeed,
To lift our heads and look up to the sky,
And think ourselves fortunate at being able to smile.

Thinking
Grant D McLeman

the chair still sits in the garden
facing the grass and the clothes-line
when it's sunny, i sit on it and read the paper
when it's raining, its seat fills with water,
and the birds take full advantage.
But on October evenings, when the autumn moon
has turned the roofs to milky custard
and the cold still is all around,
i imagine you sitting there, telescope in hand,
almanac at the ready, staring at the stars.
...it's odd to think you're part of them now.

Whipsnade Zoo
Caroline Pherozshaw

Is there a need to keep this zoo?
And imprison animals as we do.
Why pretend it's for their good.
When the animals would prefer to be free if they could!
To pretend they would die and become extinct,
Is the reason they give but that really stinks.

The animals have been led in two by two,
into their cages;
But what did they do to deserve this fate?
Oh but they did mate and produce their young,
To show everyone who comes to gloat,
And point their fingers at the apes
Who cowl in the corners.

It makes my heart break to see such misery.

But the visitors keep coming and provide the dough
And the zoo is popular so why should it go!

It's entertaining on a Saturday;
To watch the leopard snap at me.
Or perhaps more fun to see the rhino spit,
Because it's unhappy - that must be it.

I wonder how we humans would feel,
All locked up in cages of steel -
I know we would then set the animals free!
As they surely have the same rights as we.

Flat 318
Stephanie K Longson

"You can't even cry,
They will call the police.
They call this a free country,
And you can't even cry."

Silence… and then
"My country killed my husband."

Cars pass below on the busy roads.

Moans in Mother Tongue
Misunderstood
As moans of ecstasy
Yield cold and stilted jeers

From other compartments, other worlds
A few feet away.

I rise to help her
Close her windows
So no one hears the pain
Beneath her skin,
Beyond her inner walls.

Across the hall,
Death comes in an envelope,
And sorrow is bound
By laces of courteous, civilised silence
While the traffic roars below.

The Birth
Alena C B Wright

Sixteen years ago last night
You were on the way
If I'd known then what I know
I'd have pushed the other way.

The midwife was a rough old stick
My moaning made her madder
When I cried "I want a wee!"
She poked me in the bladder.

"Phone me hubby, NOW!" I yelled
"I also want me mum."
And her reply to my outcry,
a needle in me bum.

Eventually, your dad came in
just in the nick of time
"I'VE BEEN OUT ON THE BOOZE" he said
"I KNOW YOU DRUNKEN SWINE."

You found your way into the world
But not without great pain
I made myself a solemn oath
"DEFINITELY NOT AGAIN!"

Love You
Carole A Wilkinson

I love you more than words can say
I love you more from day to day
You make my life each day so sweet
With you my life is so complete.

I love you more than Apple Pie
Peaches or fresh cream
You're the only one in my life
You're the only one in my dreams.

You've also said some hurtful things
I will remember till I die
The little things that hurt deep down
The things that make you cry.

But being in love is to forgive and forget
Or so people say
I'll love you more forever and ever
I'll love you every day.

A Furry Tale
Jeremy Snooks

Across meadows and fields,
The wily creature runs,
Victim of gentry's sons,
He can't avoid the guns,
So to his pain he yields.

And so the dogs sniff 'round,
Their cousin they have caught,
'Though that capture he fought,
All in the name of sport,
He dies without a sound.

There'll be no wooden box,
No hearse, no-one to mourn,
No grave with headstone worn,
As flesh from bones is torn,
No lament for this fox.

Kiss Me Before
Daphne Wright

Kiss me before I turn into a stream
and lose myself in the great river.
For it is big and wide
mating with the tide,
and I'd be lost
vigorously tossed aside -
I being of no great matter.

Kiss me before my tears drown
you and me - and all who feel
as we do.
Feelings are immortal
though we are doomed to die.
We being but a brief reality,
a fleeting symbol of love

This Is Life
Alistair Jack

Looking around me through the vast realms of life
Everyone around me I see is black and white
thinking they've found happiness
though in reality, losing their sight
My voice rests on silence as I cry out to help them
they just cannot hear
To be truly an individual is a concept that lies
embodied in their souls as their darkest fear
Like sheep following a shepherd
they blindly follow the rest
But then how easy it makes life
when it's not even a test
The environment moulds them as a potter shapes clay
to some it's not even in the essence of their spirit
that there is another way
How weak and sad these poor creatures are
but alas what can be done for these ones
that have strayed so far?

Missing You
Doreen Chapman

Each day seems to last forever
Each night is an endless trial
The longing and the emptiness
Are with me all the while
I sometimes think I'm dreaming
And soon I will awake
It scares me when I think I'll find
Your love was just a fake
You fill my every waking thought
You're all that's on my mind
I've tried to put you in the past
And leave our love behind
Impossible as it turned out
My heart would not let go
There never really was a choice
Because I love you so
In my dreams, when I close my eyes
Safe in your arms I lay
Loving me and holding me
All these endless nights and days.

The Rumble
James Greig

There were more of us at least.
We few are some of us at most.
After all,
They dared us to go, so we did.

As usual, it was grave at least.
(it may have been worse at most)
After all,
That's why they dare us to go: Why we do.

That's why there are more of us at least, you see.
That's why we few are some of us at most. After all.

Tempus Fugit
Joy Jermy

When Age hangs heavy, like an old grey cloak
With weight, not warmth enfolding,
The restless spirit longing to be free,
Chafes at the long withholding.

Rememb'ring how there once was leaping
Into each new exciting day
But now, a slow and painful creeping,
Along a rough and stumbling way.

But still the world can offer much
Of beauty that inspires me,
The fragrant opening of a rose
The joy of children playing free.

The smile of courage on a face,
A kindness asking no reward
Are things which I could not replace,
And for them all, I thank you, Lord.

Untitled
Lydia McShane

My mother was a shuffling, shambling shell
Lost in her past life
And I cared.
I watched her painful progress down the street
Not lifting her feet
And I cared.
She no longer bathed or cooked or cleaned
Or even *saw* dirt
And so I cared.
She was my parent and my child,
Wilful, stubborn and proud.
But I still cared.
Patience turned to intolerance,
Love turned to resentment,
Compassion turned to anger
And anger gave way to guilt
So once again I cared.
I BLOODY CARED!
And wondered, "When will I live my life?"
Suddenly
She was gone and in her place
An active mother lives in my memory.
I cry and care
But cannot tell my love.

Burning The Candle Of Love
Helen Watson

A still, bright light,
Shining so sure
Against this black night.

With fiery power,
Like lovers' hearts,
You burn the twilight hour.

You're the wax to seal
The gently growing glow
That all must sometimes feel.

So why then do you cry?
For fear that, like love,
Your flame will flicker and die.

Crystal Days
David Anderson

Beneath the clouds the painting ran away
All month long. We twisted to the score,
Stood corpse-like waiting for the day
When all would gently tear.

Each saw the weeping sun go rolling home
And rise. As we stuttered to agree,
A pocket full of men began to mourn
Whilst we sheltered in the eye.

313

I spied the green come rushing from it's shell
Lend battle to the sea of fire and red. Yet,
Strangely still the throng cried out the call
To dream and not to fight.

Within the shrill the sound of night did haunt
The labelled. As they begged and scrubbed and whined
for shade,
And onwards still deceptors tried to flaunt
With scurrilous tirades.

Before the time had passed
Tomorrows born. Played daily in the warp,
And rendered dead the whining of old words
As they battled in their sleep.

The Human Race
Patricia Hunt

People rushing everywhere,
They don't have time to sit and stare
At nothing.
Too busy trying to get things done,
They don't have time for simple fun.
If only they would stop a while
And sometimes laugh or even smile,
The world might be a better place,
With humans in the human race.

I Want
Mary G Millar

I sit by the window and watch the rain fall
I want to go outside and play with my new beach ball.

I want to build a sandcastle and swim in the sea
Then gather some cockles to take home for my tea.

I want to go to the funfair and whiz down the slide
I want to go on the pier then have a boat ride.

I want an ice cream with a chocolate flake on top
I want to buy a red kite from the local beach shop.

I want to wear my sunhat with my new swim suit
When I wear it my Nan says I look really cute.

I want to dig in the sand and make my own pool
It is so much nicer than going to school.

I've come to the seaside for my holiday
And I really do want to go outside and play.

There are so many things that I want to see
But when the rain stops it will be time for tea.

If You Look
Patrick S Bainton

I hope you're happy in your world,
And have all that you could need,

But should you look around my friend,
You'll see a different world indeed.
If you look with pride my friend,
You'll see the good that has been done,
You'll hear the people singing,
Their voices raised, as if as one.
But if you look with sorrowful mind,
You will see those that life has left behind,
The ones that live in abject fear,
Surprisingly they live quite near.
If you look with pity,
My friend you'll hear their cries,
You'll see the childrens poverty,
You'll hear the officials lies.
Then if you look with anguish,
My friend perhaps you'll see,
The people living on the streets,
The ragged ones like me..
So, if you look at all my friend,
Then please, please look our way,
Don't turn your back and look elsewhere,
Because we need your help today...!

Love Dawns
D Cooper

You wake one day to normal life
to sun, - or even rain,
But ere the night has truly come
you feel a stabbing pain.
A pain so sweet - and yet it's sore
that shot from 'Cupid's' dart,

You feel the surging feeling
which arises from your heart,
A feeling which has no regard
for age, or time or place.
It happens to the young in school,
or in the years of grace.
But it is just as sharply real
this tender loving pain,
And be it fleeting, - or for life
you're not the same again.
Enriched by depth of feeling
awakened by a glance,
Your step is light, - your eyes are bright
They call this thing Romance.

Shrine
Anthony Howells

Humbled by your beauty
You tantalise
I idolise
I'm spellbound and mesmerised
Dumbstruck
I wish to say, if only I could
The words on my lips are,
"I love you".
In my mind a maze
Once an avenue of clear thoughts
My heart beats
Your kiss on my lips still smoulders
My heart skips
One day I know

You'll be gone tomorrow
Leaving just memories
Tormenting my soul
Only the ghost will remain
The ghost of our love
That can never be exorcised
Humbled
My head bowed
At the foot of the shrine
I built for you
And our lost love.

Outdoor Painting
Susan Carter

I find the view and put the easel up
And on the palette squeeze delicious paint,
Turps in an old and dully splattered cup,
Horsehair brushes lie without a taint
Of oil or turps or colours yet to come.
The canvas put on easel fiercely white,
I take a breath as if to conjure up some
Unknown force to help me in a fight,
Looking hard at what I hope to show,
The qualities of that particular site
The palette knife moves fast and seems to know
Which colours to pick up and mix aright
Viridian, titanium and red
Yellow ochre, lemon, cobalt blue.
A landscape old and yet it could be said
That as I paint, it seems to be brand new.
Sometimes it's like a passionate affair

Or taking part in some primeval race,
But other times I'm quietly made aware
The slow unfolding virtues of the place.

The light has changed and so I'll stop today
And suddenly tired put my things away.

Untitled
Marie Murphy

I met a girl today
I used to be her friend
She taught me to play marbles
And the art of the handstand
She had the world in her pocket
And life in the palm of her hand

She was gonna take the world by storm
And show them who was boss
She was the queen of the castle
No candle in the wind
Now she lives like the rest
A slave to the grind

She has a man who doesn't work
A tiny child to care for
A job to go to every morning
A house to clean every night
A girl who once had everything
Somehow it doesn't seem right

I met a girl today
I used to be her friend
She liked to laugh and clown around
Life was just a big joke
Today she was still laughing
But with bitterness that made her choke

Sun Rise
Teresa Anderson

I am magnetically drawn
To that smile
Those eyes
Like the rising sun
In soft morning skies

Can it be
For me the sun has risen
And some unseen magnetic force
Has drawn you to me
For we are in common I feel
Two spirits
Longing to fly free

Into the sun
Away from this place
It is then you will see
The sun rise
'In my face'

Life
Alison Hill

Wearily he began the steep climb.
Wistfully gazing at the dizzy heights.
Knowingly he was watched by an old woman.
Slowly she hobbled after him.
Thankfully he reached the top,
Joyously gazing over fields and forests.
Happily he turned to go.
Angrily his eye caught towering chimneys.
Blindly he pushed past the woman.
Quickly she reached out to stop him.
Softly she talked, quietly, smoothly.
Grudgingly he listened, entranced.
Mysteriously she wove a spell of life,
Sweetly whispering in cold life's sadness.
Cleverly she made him see -
Sadly, sacrifices must be made for
Happily lived lives.

Fabric Of A Dream
Dennis Carroll

Strands of reddish-gold I pluck from this one dawn -
Not quite like other dawns -
A subtle difference here and there's
A snowflake from a different day,
To sparkle sequin-like upon
The blue-green backcloth of these China Seas,
Edged with a puff of smoky grey
From the funnel of a boat that's very slow...

Across the Brahmaputra to the Naga Hills
Silent we glide by raft and winding path.
Then soar above the palace of the Khan
To float like lotus petals down the wind
And come to rest by Baghdad's Golden Mosque.

So much - and so much more - I weave
Into a Grand Mosaic
Shot through from end to end with shimmering you.
I touch your hand. The patchwork piece explodes
In cascades far and wide - and yet
It's not destroyed. It is more beautiful
Than else it was before, embracing now
A sunset touch and, in the afterglow,
A silken song breaks through.

A Special Friend
June Turner

A special friend is hard to find
It's someone who is good and kind
A precious gift and one so rare
Just someone who is always there

When times are good, they smile with glee
As we enjoy their company
Our confidence in each we share
It's nice to have - someone to care

But in the darkest of our days
They help in very many ways
Shoulder to cry on if we need
A helping hand a friend indeed

A friend is worth their weight in gold
No matter whether young or old
A listening ear through joy or strife
For true friends, are friends, all your life

Be Warned!
Helen Marlow

I remember the buzz from my first joint
Man, it was just amazing
I sat there stoned as my mind opened up
Body still, head and heart racing.

I've tried most others since that fateful day
E's, coke. smack - more than a bit
But I've now spent the last ten years of my life
Chasing that first ever hit.

Euphoria In Colour
Rachel Thomas

Sunlight
Shines its guiding light
Beams across my face
Tailight
Burst into my life
And hates my cursed face
Purple
For the violet words
You rain down on me
Scarlet

For the blood I've spilt
Silver for my tears
Yellow
Is for the summer
Blue is for the skies
Black is for the darkness
That hides a lovers eyes
Colours hold a lifetime
of pleasure and of pain
I hate every colour
When my whole world is grey

Sea Memories
G I Stephenson

The whispering ripple
of a sunsetting sea
borne in by the tide
caresses the shore.

Gazing along the sunkissed horizon
the memories of man and boy
ebb and flow
on the tides of yesteryear.

What secrets the shingle holds
as the sand dunes sing their song
beneath a leaden grey sky
on the wind of change
where the seaweed drifts on by.

Then breaks the dawn
with a thunderous roar
and the surf filled waves
carry memories no more.

Proteus
Martin Brennan

at last! the greyness descends round,
old magick's cap around the fool
and sopor's nightime lady bends
to kiss, who always thirsted more,
i have stepped out amongst these masks
among the dead and set to stone,
the yellow sign which spelt No Football
never had a captain known

- at once i fell, into the pain
my new-lit view still crossed in black,
as morning ne'er blew so strong across the final act;
and we, a hundred years from now,
this power will sustain,
when towns and roads and cities planned
are at last fucked, the biggest man,
and i was not consoled

that night, i thought a tracer linking,
in the space between the poles
and as you said *i'll role one,*
some rare sentiment did grow:
yet around me comes a steeling,
in a darkening of tone
like a tiger in an idyll,

Wanderlust
Gwen Eastwood

He who wanderlust ensnares
Can never quench that thirst;
His destination yet unknown,
His goal is ever further on:
Though he explores the whole wide world,
There is still the Great Beyond.

Belfast - Seacat - M4 - Glasgow
Tim G Noble

Sucked by foul breath of diesel slipstream shrouded spray
From Glasgow bound refrigerated articulated truck
S4725G Long Vehicle rattling tail-lights dazzle
Vice-grip knuckles wheel sweating leather
Right foot curls 'tween Brake and Death
Stiffened neck on red raw nerve ends
Strain to grip the 6pm metaphor
Of retina searing artillery fire
From frenzied multi-storey rush hour traffic
Spewed from the septic boil of some throbbing city centre

Five are-we-there-soon children
And Mary, map bedecked and kitchen rolled
Squint for hope of ill rehearsed road signs
Reduce Speed Now
Asphalt screaming rubber
End of Dual Carriage Way
Concrete reinforced steel overhead
Ring Road gawking chevrons
Coned diversion
Monoxide belching moronic klaxons and the same to you with
knobs on...

Nurtured by the sleepy spire and foggy bogs of lush and green
Fermanagh
A stubborn residue
Of what I am
Never again this screwed up insanity
I swear

The Widower
M J King

I long to take his care worn face
In these two hands of mine,
To soothe away his tiredness
Erase the lines of time.
How tall he stands and only I
Know of the load he bears,
The whitened hair, the haggard look,
Brought on by endless cares.
If I could take his sorrow now
And spirit it away,
To bring a smile to his sad eyes,
Or keep his grief at bay.
That time will pass, in passing heal,
The pain that fills his heart,
A thing that I am sure of but
When will the healing start?
He spends his days in waiting for
A door to open wide,
So he can walk that span of time,
To reach my mother's side.

Screw It
B Davies Robertson

Men can have it anytime
No regulation, it's fine
Sow your oats, screw around
Lots of women to be found
Boost your ego, tell a mate
Degrade the woman you take
Tell your stories, tell your lies
If it makes your weapon rise
Off you go, grab some action
Another victim for your satisfaction.

The Old Oak Tree
Jeanette Irwin

One day in Spring I went into the woods,
I stopped a while and there I stood,
I saw the giant oak tree,
And you'd think to see it that it had seen me.

It was about thirty metres high,
It looked as though it touched the sky,
Compared to it I seemed so small,
But the oak tree was very tall.

Its leaves were green and curvy the whole way up,
The acorn was oval and held in a sort of cup,
The bark was grey and rough,
And also very, very tough.

I went back in the winter and saw it again,
And I was glad that I had came,
I saw squirrels looking for their nuts,
And on the oak tree clusters of many scaled buds.

I visit it often, and often indeed,
To look at the leaves and examine the seeds,
It will always be my friend,
Until its life doth end.

Our Little Girl
Lesley Hartley

We waited all these months for you
Looking forward to the day
When we could share and hold you close
And love you in our special way

Making plans, such silly plans
Looking much too far ahead
Yes everything we had for you
But now just you we want instead

Never thinking things might happen
Only to others things go wrong
Now you're gone and we don't have you
The months ahead they seem so long

Feeling empty, feeling cheated
All that time and nothing to show
How I wish time could go back
Then we'd never have to know

Born so still, never moving
Not a breath did you take
Eyes that would never open
Our little girl will not awake

And if there should be babes to follow
In a future that lies so deep
You will always be our second
Little babe we couldn't keep

After The Bombing
Mark Dale

Close to the edge
and the birds are singing
World inside out
and my mind is drifting

Insanity is near
and the bodies are burning
Opinions shift
and my heart is breaking

I am falling apart
and the wind is blowing
the raindrops drop
and the clouds are shifting

Tears in my soup
and I can't stop crying
reality reigns
and my hopes are dying

Noise in my ears
and I can't stop shaking
thoughts of tomorrow
and of how I'm living.

The Owl
Tanja Moston

The owl whom we know is a bird of prey,
he hunts at night and sleeps in the day.

Mice hide away in their snug little nests,
while the owl looks for food he's trying his best.

After a while he sees a curious hole,
he wonders if inside hides a mouse or a vole.

He looks inside and guess what he sees,
such a disappointment it's a nest full of bees!

Then when the owl is about to give up,
he sees something moving could it be luck?

It is, there's some mice it looks like a family,
then as quick as a flash he flies to a tall tree.

Then he circles down and spreads out his claws,
and grabs the mice till there are no more.

The Rubbish Collector
Eamonn Costello

There once was an old man we used to know
He lived nearby just down the road
Every day he collected old toys and rags
Some say his house was filled with big red bags
Now this old man had some boys
All through the night making lots of noise
In the day when he went out
The house fell silent not a shout
This old man was very very old
A long white beard and a heart of gold
When December comes and the first falls of snow
The old man would disappear and go
He loves the children so very much
This old man never loses touch
I do not know where he goes
But I bet the kids hear his sleigh bells.

I Remember
Kath Speck

I remember my mother, sat in her chair as she would
sometimes do.
Limpid, smiling eyes of greyish blue.
I know, I was glad that she was always there,
Ready, if you had a trouble or a laugh to share.

She was always such a busy bee,
Doing things for everybody, including me.
She never complained, or seemed sad.
Always happy with what she had.

She liked other people, and often you'd see
Her working hard for some charity.
She made everyone welcome and the first thing she'd do
Was to pop on the kettle for a cuppa for you.

She loved gardening, nature and animals too
There seemed no end to the facts that she knew.
She taught us all to knit, to cook and to sew,
And lots and lots of other things that we all now know.

Then one long, unforgettable day,
A cruel stroke took her 'away'.
Six days in a hospital bed she lay,
I hoped and prayed she would be ok.

But, God knows why, this was not to be
She's gone forever, from you and me.
I miss her, it hurts to know she's not there
I'll always remember how much I loved her.

Changing Seasons
Maura Maguire

The countryside in autumn is beautiful to behold
Lavish colours intermingled, russet red and gold
The ripening fruits add colour to the ever changing scene
And twirling leaves bedeck the path
Then play in joyous mien.

This now fair scene alas must change
To usher the dreary day
Which proclaims approaching winter

Making fast its onward way
The mellow sun grows paler
The colours fade away
But winter has its rightful place
And dons its drab array

Pause
Danielle Fawcett

I'm constantly on fast forward
Sometimes even on rewind
But somewhere in between
Lies a happy medium
Perhaps I'd like to find.
I feel old, although I'm not
My reel is always spinning
And I'm walking through endless open doors
If it was perfectly natural
Would someone please press pause.

Untitled
John Jones

The frail old man just got to his seat,
Before the bus, set off down the street,
The bus driver laughed, "Look what I've done,
I've made the old man fall down on his bum",
The old man was cursing, he'd come to expect,
That kind of treatment from that kind of sect.

Now this frail old man, I thought I should mention,
Was only going out to pick up his pension,
And to get some bread and cheese for his lunch,
And gaze at some flowers at 30p a bunch,
He thought of those people, in that same street,
Who spent more on flowers, than he did on meat.

He wishes he had enough money to spare,
To go for a drink in the pub over there,
But buying a pint is terribly risky,
He wouldn't stop there, he'd go for a whisky,
So he goes without, to make sure he's able,
To have some bread and cheese on the table.

I know this old man, he's somewhere 'upstairs',
Nobody knows him - nobody cares,
I'll put it into words if I can,
I'd hate to be like that frail old man,
The truth of the matter, if you have to be told,
It frightens me that, I too will grow old.